DATA SCIENCE FOR
DECISION MAKERS

DATA SCIENCE FOR DECISION MAKERS

Using Analytics and Case Studies

Erik Herman

MERCURY LEARNING AND INFORMATION
Boston, Massachusetts

Publisher: David Pallai
Mercury Learning and Information
121 High Street, 3rd Floor
Boston, MA 02110
info@merclearning.com
www.merclearning.com
800-232-0223

E. Herman. *Data Science for Decision Makers: Using Analytics and Case Studies.*
ISBN: 978-1-50152-331-1

The publisher recognizes and respects all marks used by companies, manufacturers, and developers as a means to distinguish their products. All brand names and product names mentioned in this book are trademarks or service marks of their respective companies. Any omission or misuse (of any kind) of service marks or trademarks, etc. is not an attempt to infringe on the property of others.

Library of Congress Control Number: 2024946867
242526321   This book is printed on acid-free paper in the United States of America.

Our titles are available for adoption, license, or bulk purchase by institutions, corporations, etc. For additional information, please contact the Customer Service Dept. at 800-232-0223(toll free).

All of our titles are available in digital format at various digital vendors. *Companion files for this title are available with proof of purchase by contacting info@merclearning.com.* The sole obligation of Mercury Learning and Information to the purchaser is to replace the files, based on defective materials or faulty workmanship, but not based on the operation or functionality of the product.

To my two beauties, Julian, and Alexandra.

CONTENTS

Preface   *xv*

Chapter 1: Understanding the Role of Data
in Business Strategy   1

Introduction to Data-Driven Decision-Making   2
    Identify market trends and consumer preferences   2
    Enhance operational efficiency   2
    Mitigate risks and uncertainties   3
    Drive innovation and competitive advantage   3
The Data Science Lifecycle   3
    Data Acquisition   3
    Data Preparation   4
    Exploratory Data Analysis (EDA)   4
    Model Development   4
    Model Evaluation   4
    Deployment and Monitoring   4
Key Concepts and Terminology   5
    Data   5
    Big Data   5
    Data Types   5
    Descriptive vs. Inferential Statistics   5
    Machine Learning   5
    Predictive Analytics   5
    Data Visualization   6
    Algorithm   6
Using Analytics: Business Strategy   6
    Strategic Decision Support   6
    Lifecycle Optimization   6
    Conceptual Understanding   7
Case Study: Optimizing Supply Chain Operations   7
    Objective   7
    Approach   7

Result   7
Sample Visualizations   8
Python code   10
Implementation Roadmap: Introduction to Data Science and
Decision Making   11
    Roadmap steps   11
Conclusion   13

Chapter 2: Foundations of Data Science   15

Data Collection: The Backbone of Data Science   16
    Data Source   16
    Data Acquisition Techniques   17
    Data Quality and Integrity   17
Data Preprocessing: Cleaning and Transforming Raw Data   17
    Data Cleaning   17
    Data Transformation   18
    Data Integration   18
Unveiling Insights Through Exploratory Data Analysis   18
    Descriptive Statistics   18
    Data Visualization   19
    Correlation Analysis   19
    Clustering and Dimensionality Reduction   19
Statistical Fundamentals for Data Analysis   20
    Probability Distributions   20
    Hypothesis Testing   20
    Regression Analysis   20
    Statistical Inference   21
Using Analytics: Data Science Foundations   21
    Data Quality Assurance   21
    Pattern Recognition   21
    Inference and Prediction   22
Case Study: Predictive Maintenance in Manufacturing   22
    Objective   22
    Approach   23
    Result   23
    Example Visualizations   24
    Python Code   25
Implementation Roadmap: Foundations of Data Science   26
    Roadmap Steps   26
Conclusion   29

Chapter 3: Data Visualization and Communication   31

Principles of Data Visualization   32
    Clarity and Simplicity   32
    Accuracy and Integrity   32

Relevance and Context   33
Use of Color and Visual Elements   33
Interactivity and Engagement   33
Tools and Techniques for Data Visualization   33
Data Visualization Libraries   33
Business Intelligence (BI) Tools   34
Geographic Information Systems (GIS)   34
Infographics and Data Storytelling   34
Dashboard Design Principles   34
Effective Data Communication Strategies   35
Know Your Audience   35
Tell a Story   35
Use Multiple Channels   35
Solicit Feedback   35
Foster Data Literacy   36
Using Analytics: Data Visualization and Communication   36
Insights Communication   36
Interactive Exploration   36
Storytelling and Persuasion   36
Case Study: Market Trend Analysis for Retail Expansion   37
Objective   37
Approach   38
Result   38
Sample Visualizations   39
Python code   40
Implementation Roadmap: Data Visualization and Communication   41
Roadmap steps: 41
Conclusion   43

Chapter 4: Predictive Analytics and Machine Learning   45

Introduction to Predictive Modeling   46
Problem Formulation   46
Data Preparation   46
Model Selection   47
Model Training   47
Model Evaluation   47
Model Deployment   47
Supervised and Unsupervised Learning Techniques   47
Supervised Learning   47
Unsupervised Learning   48
Model Evaluation and Validation   48
Performance Metrics   49
Cross-Validation   49
Model Selection   49

Validation Strategies   49
Overfitting and Underfitting   49
Using Analytics: Predictive Analytics and Machine Learning   50
Predictive Modeling   50
Unsupervised Learning   50
Model Evaluation and Validation   50
Case Study: Personalized Recommendations in E-commerce   50
Objective   51
Approach   52
Result   52
Sample Visualizations   52
Python Code   54
Implementation Roadmap: Predictive Analytics and Machine Learning   54
Roadmap Steps   55
Conclusion   57

Chapter 5: Ethical Considerations in Data Science   **59**
Ethics in Data Collection and Usage   60
Privacy and Consent   60
Data Ownership and Control   60
Data Security   61
Responsible Data Usage   61
Fairness, Bias, and Transparency   61
Fairness in Algorithm Design   61
Bias Detection and Mitigation   61
Transparency and Explainability   62
Algorithmic Impact Assessments   62
Legal and Regulatory Frameworks   62
Data Protection Laws   62
Anti-Discrimination Laws   62
Intellectual Property Rights   63
Regulatory Compliance   63
Using Analytics: Ethical Considerations in Data Science   63
Ethical Data Collection and Usage   63
Fairness, Bias, and Transparency   63
Compliance with Legal and Regulatory Frameworks   64
Case Study: Fair Lending Practices in Financial Services   64
Objective   65
Approach   65
Result   65
Sample Visualizations   66
Python Code   68
Implementation Roadmap: Ethical Considerations in Data Science   69
Roadmap Steps   69
Conclusion   71

Chapter 6: Building a Data-Driven Culture   73

Fostering a Culture of Data Literacy   74
    Education and Training   74
    Promote Continuous Learning   75
    Firsthand Experience   75
    Leadership Support   75
Overcoming Organizational Challenges   75
    Change Management   75
    Data Integration and Governance   75
    Resource Allocation   76
    Metrics and KPIs   76
Implementing Data-Driven Decision Making   76
    Define Clear Objectives   76
    Data Collection and Analysis   76
    Decision Support Systems   77
    Iterative Improvement   77
    Cultivate a Learning Culture   77
Using Analytics: Building a Data-Driven Culture   77
    Fostering a Culture of Data Literacy   77
    Overcoming Organizational Challenges   77
    Implementing Data-Driven Decision Making   78
Case Study: Cultivating Data Literacy in a Healthcare Organization   78
    Objective   79
    Approach   79
    Result   79
    Sample Visualizations   80
    Python Code   82
Implementation Roadmap: Building a Data-Driven Culture   82
    Roadmap Steps   83
Conclusion   85

Chapter 7: Case Studies in Data-Driven Success   87

Industry-Specific Case Studies   88
    Retail   88
    Healthcare   89
    Finance   89
    Manufacturing   89
    Marketing   90
Lessons Learned and Best Practices   90
    Data Quality and Governance   90
    Cross-Functional Collaboration   90
    Agile and Iterative Approach   91
    Ethical Considerations   91
Practical Insights for Decision Makers   91
    Leadership Support   91

Talent Acquisition and Development 91
Measure Impact and ROI 92
Continuous Improvement 92
Using Analytics: Case Studies in Data-Driven Success 92
Industry-Specific Case Studies 92
Lessons Learned 92
Best Practices 93
Case Study Compilation: Lessons from Industry-Specific Data
Successes 93
Industry-Specific Case Studies 93
Lessons Learned and Best Practices 94
Implementation Roadmap: Case Studies in Data-Driven Success 96
Roadmap Steps 96
Conclusion 99

Chapter 8: The Future of Data Analytics **101**
Emerging Trends Shaping the Future of Data Analytics 101
Advanced AI and Machine Learning (ML) 101
Real-Time Analytics and Edge Computing 102
Augmented Analytics 102
Automated Machine Learning (AutoML) 103
Data Ethics, Privacy, and Governance 103
Technological Advancements Impacting Data Analytics 103
Quantum Computing 103
Blockchain Technology for Data Integrity 104
Advanced Data Visualization Tools 104
Internet of Things (IoT) and Connected Devices 104
The Evolution of Data-Driven Decision Making 105
Conclusion 105
Embracing Technological Advancements for a Competitive
Edge 105
The Role of Ethics and Data Governance in the Future of
Analytics 105
Data as a Strategic Asset 106
Building a Data-Driven Culture 106
Anticipating the Challenges and Preparing for the Future 106
Toward a Future Where Data is Central to Every Industry 107
Empowering Decision-Makers with Data-Driven Insights 107
Data Analytics as a Path to Innovation and Growth 107

Chapter 9: Getting Started with Data Analytics
Development **109**
Setting Up a Data Analytics Development Environment 109
Choosing and Installing Python as the Primary Language 110
Selecting the Right IDE 110

Hardware Considerations for Data Processing 110
Introduction to Python for Data Analytics 111
Essential Libraries for Data Analytics 111
Practical Application: Setting Up a Data Analytics Environment
and Running an Initial Analysis 112
Step-by-Step Guide to Setting Up and Running an Analysis 112
Example Script: Loading and Visualizing Data 113
Conclusion 113

Appendix A: Glossary of Key Terms 115
Appendix B: Ethical Considerations Framework 121
Appendix C: Python Code Files 125
Appendix D: Data Sets 131
Appendix E: 100 Luminaries in Data Science 157
Appendix F: Top 10 Data-Driven Decisions 165
Index 171

*P*REFACE

Data Science for Decision Makers: Using Analytics and Case Studies simplifies the complex world of data science, making it accessible and actionable for business leaders. This book emphasizes the essential role of data in making informed decisions that drive business success. Through clear explanations, practical applications, and detailed case studies, it equips readers with the tools and knowledge needed to navigate today's data-driven business environment.

The text begins by introducing the fundamentals of data-driven decision-making, demonstrating how data can uncover market trends, enhance operational efficiencies, drive innovation, and establish competitive advantages. It covers the entire data science lifecycle, including data acquisition, preparation, analysis, model development, evaluation, and deployment, ensuring readers grasp each stage essential for effective data analysis.

Each chapter builds upon these foundational concepts with real-world applications and comprehensive case studies. These case studies highlight practical data science solutions, featuring sample data sets, visualizations, and Python code, providing a hands-on approach for readers to directly apply what they learn.

The book also explores ethical considerations in data usage, addressing topics such as privacy, bias, transparency, and compliance. It emphasizes the need for building a data-driven culture within organizations and outlines strategies to foster data literacy, collaboration, and continuous improvement.

CHAPTER 1: UNDERSTANDING THE ROLE OF DATA IN BUSINESS STRATEGY

This chapter discusses the strategic importance of data in modern business, explaining how organizations can use data to identify opportunities, optimize operations, and maintain a competitive edge. It emphasizes aligning data strategies with business goals and integrating data insights into decision-making processes.

CHAPTER 2: FOUNDATIONS OF DATA SCIENCE

Covering the core principles of data science, this chapter walks readers through the data science lifecycle, including data acquisition, preparation, and exploration. It introduces essential statistical methods, programming basics, and data wrangling techniques, laying a solid foundation for more advanced topics.

CHAPTER 3: DATA VISUALIZATIONS AND COMMUNICATION

This chapter focuses on effectively communicating insights through data visualizations. It explores best practices for creating impactful charts, using storytelling with data, and tailoring visual presentations for different audiences to ensure that decision-makers can effectively interpret and act on analytical findings.

CHAPTER 4: PREDICTIVE ANALYTICS AND MACHINE LEARNING

Here, readers are introduced to predictive analytics and common machine learning algorithms for forecasting and classification. The chapter covers model development, training, evaluation, and validation, using case studies and practical exercises to demonstrate applications like sales forecasting and customer segmentation.

CHAPTER 5: ETHICAL CONSIDERATIONS IN DATA SCIENCE

This chapter addresses the ethical challenges associated with data science, including privacy, bias, transparency, and compliance. It emphasizes the need for businesses to establish frameworks that ensure responsible and fair data practices.

CHAPTER 6: BUILDING A DATA-DRIVEN CULTURE

Emphasizing the importance of fostering a data-driven culture, this chapter explores strategies for enhancing data literacy, promoting cross-departmental collaboration, and implementing tools and platforms that support data initiatives. It highlights the role of leadership in creating an environment where data is valued.

CHAPTER 7: CASE STUDIES IN DATA-DRIVEN SUCCESS

The final chapter brings together all the concepts discussed throughout the book through real-world case studies from various industries. These cases illustrate how data science can solve business challenges, improve operations, and drive innovation. Each case study includes sample data, visualizations, and Python code, providing readers with hands-on examples of data science applications.

CHAPTER 8: THE FUTURE OF DATA ANALYTICS

This chapter explores the transformative trends shaping the future of data analytics, such as advanced artificial intelligence, edge computing, augmented analytics, and quantum computing. It discusses the shift from traditional, retrospective analysis to real-time, predictive, and prescriptive analytics. By understanding these advancements, readers can anticipate industry changes and strategically integrate emerging analytics capabilities to maintain a competitive edge.

CHAPTER 9: GETTING STARTED WITH DATA ANALYTICS DEVELOPMENT

Providing a practical guide to setting up a data analytics environment, this chapter covers essential tools and best practices for working with Python, setting up Integrated Development Environments (IDEs) like Jupyter Notebook, and using libraries for data manipulation, visualization, and modeling. Readers are equipped to create a productive setup tailored to the needs of data analytics, supporting tasks from data preparation to advanced analysis.

The appendices offer additional resources that enhance the book's practical value:

Appendix A: Glossary of Key Terms – Provides a glossary of essential data science terms, serving as a quick reference for readers to better understand technical concepts throughout the book.

Appendix B: Ethical Considerations Framework – Offers a structured framework for evaluating ethical implications in data science projects, covering privacy, fairness, and transparency to guide responsible data practices.

Appendix C: Python Code Files – Contains Python code files used in the book, allowing readers to access, modify, and execute code examples independently to reinforce learning.

Appendix D: Data Sets – A collection of diverse datasets, including business sales, retail transactions, pollution levels, housing prices, and credit risk assessment, designed for hands-on practice in areas like trend identification, predictive modeling, and segmentation.

Appendix E: 100 Luminaries in Data Science – A list of influential figures in data science, statistics, machine learning, and data visualization. This appendix offers readers insights into the contributions of key figures who have shaped the field, from pioneers like John Tukey to modern leaders like Geoffrey Hinton.

Appendix F: Top 10 Data-Driven Decisions – Examples of impactful, data-driven decisions from industry leaders such as Google, Amazon, and Netflix. Each example illustrates how strategic data use transformed industries and improved business outcomes, demonstrating the real-world impact of analytics.

Data Science for Decision Makers serves not just as a technical manual but as a strategic guide for leaders looking to harness the power of data analytics in their decision-making processes. It offers business professionals the insights and strategies necessary to transform their organizational practices and lead confidently in a data-centric world.

Companion Files

This text is supported by a comprehensive set of resources designed to enhance learning and provide hands-on practice for readers. Below is an overview of the accompanying files:

1. Python Scripts

The Python scripts provided with this book are tailored to reinforce the concepts and techniques discussed in the chapters. These scripts include:

- **Data Cleaning and Preprocessing**: Scripts demonstrating techniques like handling missing values, data normalization, and feature engineering.
- **Exploratory Data Analysis (EDA)**: Sample code for creating descriptive statistics, histograms, scatter plots, and other visualization techniques.
- **Machine Learning Models**: Ready-to-use scripts for building predictive models, including linear regression, logistic regression, random forests, and neural networks.
- **Visualization Examples**: Code showcasing data visualization libraries like Matplotlib, Seaborn, and Plotly for creating publication-ready charts and dashboards.
- **Case Studies**: End-to-end implementations of case studies discussed in the book, including data loading, cleaning, analysis, modeling, and interpretation.

2. Data Files

A variety of datasets are included to allow readers to practice the methods described in the text. These datasets cover a range of industries and analysis types:

- **Sales and Marketing Data**: A dataset simulating sales trends, marketing spend, and product performance.
- **Customer Transactions**: Retail transaction data for analysis of purchasing patterns and customer segmentation.
- **City Pollution Levels**: Environmental data on pollution, temperature, and population density for time series analysis.
- **Housing Prices**: A real estate dataset including property features and sale prices for regression analysis.
- **Credit Risk Assessment**: Financial data for modeling loan approvals and defaults.
- **Employee Engagement**: Survey results on employee satisfaction and engagement for clustering and predictive analysis.

All datasets are provided in CSV format for easy integration with Python and other tools.

3. Color Images

High-quality color images from the text are included to help readers visualize complex data and concepts. These images feature:

- **Data Visualizations**: Examples of bar charts, scatter plots, heatmaps, and dashboards used in the text.
- **Illustrative Diagrams**: Flowcharts, machine learning pipeline diagrams, and data process visualizations.
- **Case Study Results**: Visual representations of findings from case studies, including predictive model outputs and performance metrics.

These images are provided in PNG format, ensuring clarity for presentations or further analysis.

How to Use These Resources

Readers can:

1. **Run Python Scripts**: Follow along with the book by executing scripts in a Python environment such as Jupyter Notebook or VS Code.

2. **Explore Data**: Load the provided datasets to practice cleaning, exploring, and modeling data.

3. **Reference Visuals**: Use the color images to better understand the concepts and replicate them in your own projects.

Together, these files create a hands-on, interactive experience, allowing readers to move from theory to application effectively. Files are available for downloading (with proof of purchase) by writing to *info@merclearning.com.*

Acknowledgments

I'd like to acknowledge anyone and everyone in pursuit of an authentic existence, be it in business, love, or life. May the data be with you.

Erik Herman
December 2024

## CHAPTER 1

Understanding the Role of Data in Business Strategy

I n the contemporary business landscape, data has emerged as a cornerstone of strategic decision-making, often referred to as the new oil for its transformative potential. The era of relying solely on intuition or limited information is over; today, organizations harness the power of big data and advanced analytics to drive growth, innovation, and competitive advantage.

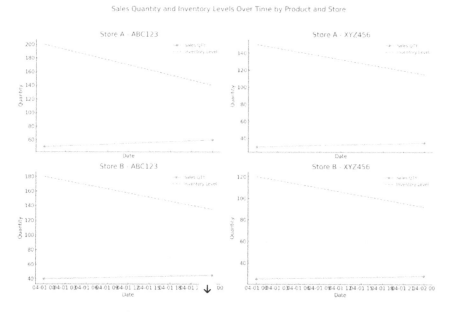

FIGURE 1.1. Sales quantity and inventory levels over time by product and store.

Figure 1.1 is a line chart showing the sales quantity and inventory levels over time for each product at each store location. This visualization demonstrates how these two metrics interact and change over the dates provided, highlighting trend shifts.

This chapter explores the pivotal role of data in shaping business strategy, illuminating how data-driven decision-making enables organizations to identify market trends, enhance operational efficiency, mitigate risks, and drive innovation. By leveraging data as a strategic asset, businesses can unlock valuable insights, gain a deeper understanding of their customers and markets, and make informed decisions that propel them toward success.

At the heart of data-driven decision-making lies the *data science lifecycle*, a systematic approach to extracting insights and value from data. This chapter provides a comprehensive overview of the data science lifecycle, spanning key stages from *data acquisition and preparation* to *exploratory data analysis, model development, evaluation, deployment*, and *monitoring*.

Through each stage of the lifecycle, organizations embark on a journey of discovery, harnessing the power of data to uncover patterns, insights, and opportunities that inform strategic decisions and drive business outcomes. Additionally, this chapter explores fundamental concepts and terminology essential for navigating the field of data science and decision-making, empowering individuals to effectively leverage data-driven approaches to achieve their organizational objectives.

With a solid understanding of the role of data in business strategy and the tools and techniques of data science at their disposal, organizations can chart a course toward success in an increasingly data-driven world.

INTRODUCTION TO DATA-DRIVEN DECISION-MAKING

The strategic approach known as data-driven decision-making underpins the ability of a company to adapt, innovate, and outperform rivals. Key to this methodology are the following foundational principles:

Identify market trends and consumer preferences

By analyzing large datasets, businesses can uncover valuable insights into market trends, consumer behavior, and emerging opportunities. This enables companies to tailor their marketing strategies, develop targeted products, and respond proactively to changing customer demands, thereby enhancing their market positioning and achieving higher customer satisfaction.

Enhance operational efficiency

Data analytics can optimize business processes, improve resource allocation, and streamline operations, leading to cost savings and increased productivity. By automating routine tasks and predicting future needs, businesses can allocate resources more effectively, reduce waste, and maximize the efficiency of their operations, contributing to a leaner, more agile organization.

Mitigate risks and uncertainties

Through predictive analytics and risk modeling, organizations can anticipate potential challenges, identify vulnerabilities, and implement initiative-taking measures to mitigate risks. This proactive approach allows companies to minimize potential losses, enhance decision-making processes, and maintain a robust strategy against the unpredictable elements of their business environments.

Drive innovation and competitive advantage

Data-driven insights empower businesses to innovate products and services, differentiate themselves in the marketplace, and stay ahead of competitors. By leveraging unique data insights, companies can discover new market niches, develop pioneering technologies, and offer enhanced customer experiences, thus establishing a strong competitive edge in their respective industries.

THE DATA SCIENCE LIFECYCLE

The data science lifecycle (*Figure 1.2*) represents the end-to-end process of extracting value from data, encompassing various stages from data collection to deployment. This iterative and comprehensive process involves multiple steps that are crucial for deriving actionable insights and achieving business outcomes. While specific methodologies may vary, the following stages are commonly observed in the data science lifecycle:

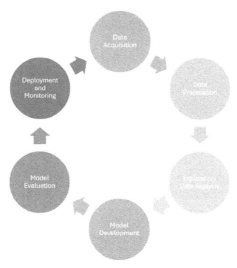

FIGURE 1.2. The data science lifecycle.

Data Acquisition

This stage involves collecting relevant data from various sources, including internal databases, external APIs, sensor networks, and social media platforms.

Effective data acquisition strategies are critical for ensuring a comprehensive dataset that accurately represents the phenomena under study. Techniques such as Web scraping, real-time data streaming, and batch data loading are often employed to gather diverse data types.

Data Preparation

Once the data is collected, it needs to be cleaned, transformed, and pre-processed to ensure its quality and suitability for analysis. This may involve tasks such as data cleaning, feature engineering, and normalization. Proper data preparation enhances the accuracy and efficiency of the models by addressing issues like missing values, outliers, and inconsistent data formats, which are critical for reliable analysis.

Exploratory Data Analysis (EDA)

EDA involves exploring and visualizing the data to gain a deeper understanding of its characteristics, patterns, and relationships. Descriptive statistics, data visualization techniques, and exploratory techniques such as clustering and dimensionality reduction are commonly used in this stage. EDA helps identify trends, test assumptions, and formulate hypotheses for further analysis, providing a solid foundation for model building.

Model Development

In this stage, statistical and machine learning models are developed to extract insights or make predictions based on the data. This may involve selecting appropriate algorithms, training and evaluating models, and tuning hyperparameters for optimal performance. Successful model development requires a thorough understanding of the underlying data and the problem context in order to choose the most effective modeling techniques.

Model Evaluation

Once the models are trained, they need to be evaluated using appropriate metrics to assess their performance and generalization capabilities. This helps ensure that the models are dependable and effective in real-world scenarios. Techniques such as cross-validation, ROC curves, and confusion matrices are crucial for evaluating model robustness and preventing issues like overfitting.

Deployment and Monitoring

The final stage involves deploying the models into production environments and monitoring their performance over time. This may include setting up automated pipelines, integrating models with existing systems, and implementing mechanisms for monitoring and feedback. Continuous monitoring is essential to quickly identify and address any performance degradation or anomalies in the models, ensuring they remain effective and accurate over time.

KEY CONCEPTS AND TERMINOLOGY

To effectively navigate the field of data science and decision-making, it is essential to understand key concepts and terminology. Some of the fundamental concepts include:

Data

Raw facts, figures, and statistics were collected for analysis. This information serves as the foundational elements for research and decision-making in various fields. Effective management, cleansing, and structuring of data are essential to ensuring its usability and relevance for specific analytical purposes.

Big Data

Large and complex data sets that exceed the processing capabilities of traditional database systems. Big Data is characterized by its volume, velocity, and variety, requiring specialized technologies and analytical methods such as Hadoop and cloud-based analytics to extract meaningful information efficiently.

Data Types

Data can be categorized into several types, including numerical (e.g., integers, floats), categorical (e.g., text, labels), ordinal (e.g., rankings), and temporal (e.g., timestamps). Understanding the nature of data types is crucial for selecting appropriate analytical techniques and models. Proper handling of these data types ensures the accuracy and effectiveness of the data analysis processes.

Descriptive vs. Inferential Statistics

Descriptive statistics involve summarizing and visualizing data to describe its key characteristics, such as mean, median, variance, and distribution. In contrast, inferential statistics involve making inferences or predictions about a population based on sample data. These statistical approaches are fundamental to research and decision-making, providing insights that guide strategic planning and policy development.

Machine Learning

Machine learning is a subset of artificial intelligence that focuses on developing algorithms and models that can learn from data and make predictions or decisions without being explicitly programmed. It encompasses various techniques, including supervised learning, unsupervised learning, and reinforcement learning. This dynamic field is pivotal in the development of systems that improve their performance iteratively as more data becomes available.

Predictive Analytics

Predictive analytics involves using historical data and statistical techniques to forecast future events or outcomes. It enables businesses to anticipate trends, identify patterns, and make initiative-taking decisions to achieve desired outcomes. This proactive approach to data analysis helps organizations optimize operations, enhance customer satisfaction, and drive innovation.

Data Visualization

Data visualization is the graphical representation of data to facilitate understanding, exploration, and communication of insights. It includes techniques such as charts, graphs, heatmaps, and interactive dashboards to present complex data in a visually appealing and accessible manner. Effective data visualization is crucial for conveying complex information quickly and enabling stakeholders to make informed decisions based on data insights.

Algorithm

A set of rules or instructions designed to solve a specific problem or perform a particular task. Algorithms are fundamental in computing and data analysis, guiding the systematic execution of operations to achieve intended results. Their design and optimization play a critical role in enhancing the efficiency and accuracy of automated processes and intelligent systems.

USING ANALYTICS: BUSINESS STRATEGY

This section focuses on the strategic utilization of business analytics, highlighting their efficacy in addressing complex challenges and driving informed decision-making, including:

Strategic Decision Support

Use analytics to understand the role of data in shaping business strategy. By analyzing historical data and market trends, businesses can gain insights into consumer behavior, market dynamics, and the competitive landscape, enabling informed strategic decision-making. This analytical approach aids organizations in identifying opportunities for growth and areas for improvement, supporting the development of strategies that are both responsive and proactive in nature. It helps in aligning business goals with market realities, ensuring that strategic initiatives are data-driven and grounded in real-world evidence.

Lifecycle Optimization

Utilize analytics throughout the data science lifecycle to optimize processes and maximize efficiency. From data collection and preprocessing to modeling and interpretation, analytics techniques such as data visualization, predictive modeling, and statistical analysis can streamline workflows and improve outcomes at each stage. This continuous optimization not only enhances the quality and speed of data processing but also increases the accuracy and relevancy of the results. By integrating analytics deeply into each phase of the data science lifecycle, organizations can achieve more consistent and scalable results, driving innovation and competitive advantage.

Conceptual Understanding

Leverage analytics to grasp key concepts and terminology essential for effective decision-making. By applying analytics tools and techniques to real-world scenarios, individuals can deepen their understanding of data science principles and their practical applications, enhancing their ability to interpret and utilize data effectively in decision-making processes. This enriched knowledge base empowers professionals to make more informed decisions, foster a data-centric culture within their organizations, and tackle complex problems with confidence. Through practical exposure to analytics, individuals can bridge the gap between theoretical knowledge and its application, facilitating better communication and strategic alignment across various levels of the organization.

CASE STUDY: OPTIMIZING SUPPLY CHAIN OPERATIONS

In the bustling world of retail, staying ahead of demand while managing inventory efficiently is paramount. Let us explore how *a leading retail chain* leveraged data science to streamline its supply chain operations and enhance decision-making.

Objective

A *leading retail chain* recognized that data held the key to unlocking insights into consumer behavior, demand patterns, and inventory management. By integrating data-driven strategies into their business model, they aimed to optimize every aspect of their supply chain, from procurement to distribution.

Approach

The *retail chain* embarked on a comprehensive data science journey, starting with data collection from various sources, including sales transactions, inventory levels, and market trends. They then moved to data preprocessing, cleaning, and transforming it into actionable insights. Using advanced analytics techniques, such as predictive modeling and clustering, they identified demand patterns and optimized inventory levels accordingly. Finally, they implemented data visualization tools to communicate insights effectively across departments.

Result

Throughout the process, *the retail chain* team familiarized themselves with key data science concepts and terminology, such as machine learning algorithms, regression analysis, and data visualization techniques. By understanding these concepts, they were able to interpret the results accurately and make informed decisions.

TABLE 1.1. Retail supply chain operations data.

Date	Store	Location	Product ID	Sales QTY	Inventory Level	Market Trends
4/1/2024	Store	A	ABC123	50	200	Stable
4/1/2024	Store	A	XYZ456	30	150	Stable
4/1/2024	Store	B	ABC123	40	180	Stable
4/1/2024	Store	B	XYZ456	25	120	Stable
4/2/2024	Store	A	ABC123	60	140	Increasing
4/2/2024	Store	A	XYZ456	35	115	Increasing
4/2/2024	Store	B	ABC123	45	135	Increasing
4/2/2024	Store	B	XYZ456	28	92	Increasing

This dataset includes:

- *Date:* The date of sales transactions or inventory updates.
- *Store Location*: The location of the store where the transaction or inventory update occurred.
- *Product ID*: A unique identifier for each product.
- *Sales Quantity*: The quantity of the product sold on that date.
- *Inventory Level*: The remaining inventory level of the product after sales or updates.
- *Market Trends*: Information on market trends that may affect demand, categorized as stable, increasing, or decreasing.

Sample Visualizations

Sales Quantity vs. Inventory Level by Product ID and Store

This scatter plot (*Figure 1.3*) shows the relationship between inventory levels and sales quantities for various products at each store. It helps in visualizing how inventory management correlates with sales performance.

FIGURE 1.3. Sales quantities vs. inventory levels by product ID and store.

Sales Quantity Trends over Time

This line graph (*Figure 1.4*) depicts the sales quantities for various products at each store over the two days. It includes changes in market trends, indicated by shifts from stable to increasing sales.

FIGURE 1.4. Inventory levels by store and product over time.

Comparison of Inventory Levels by Store and Product over Time

Another line graph (*Figure 1.5*) displays how inventory levels changed over the same period. This can be useful for understanding how stores adjust their inventories in response to sales trends and market conditions.

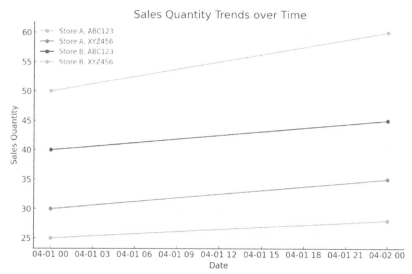

FIGURE 1.5. Sales quantity trends over time.

Python code

```
1   import pandas as pd
2   import seaborn as sns
3   import matplotlib.pyplot as plt
4
5   # Data setup
6   data_1 = {
7   "Date": ["4/1/2024", "4/1/2024", "4/1/2024", "4/1/2024", "4/2/2024", "4/2/2024", "4/2/2024", "4/2/2024"],
8   "Store": ["Store A", "Store A", "Store B", "Store B", "Store A", "Store A", "Store B", "Store B"],
9   "Product ID": ["ABC123", "XYZ456", "ABC123", "XYZ456", "ABC123", "XYZ456", "ABC123", "XYZ456"],
10  "Sales QTY": [50, 30, 40, 25, 60, 35, 45, 28],
11  "Inventory Level": [200, 150, 180, 120, 140, 115, 135, 92]
12  }
13
14  df_1 = pd.DataFrame(data_1)
15  # Visualization 1: Sales Quantity by Store and Date
16  plt.figure(figsize=(10, 6))
17  sns.lineplot(data=df_1, x='Date', y='Sales QTY', hue='Store', style='Store', markers=True, dashes=False)
18  plt.title('Sales Quantity by Store and Date')
19  plt.show()
20
21  # Visualization 2: Inventory Levels by Store and Date
22  plt.figure(figsize=(10, 6))
23  sns.lineplot(data=df_1, x='Date', y='Inventory Level', hue='Store', style='Store', markers=True, dashes=False)
24  plt.title('Inventory Levels by Store and Date')
25  plt.show()
```

FIGURE 1.6. An example of Python code.

This Python script (*Figure 1.6*) uses the "Pandas™," "Seaborn™," and "Matplotlib™" libraries for data manipulation and visualization:

- *Imports*: The script begins by importing the necessary libraries. "Pandas" is used for creating and handling data in DataFrame format, "seaborn" for high-level statistical graphics, and "matplotlib.pyplot" for plot customization.
- *Data Setup*: The data, including dates, store names, product IDs, sales quantities, and inventory levels, is organized into a dictionary and then converted into a pandas DataFrame. This structure allows for easier data manipulation.
- *Visualization 1*: Sales Quantity by Store and Date: A line plot is created showing sales quantity over time, differentiated by store. It features markers on each data point and uses solid lines for distinction.
- *Visualization 2*: Inventory Levels by Store and Date: Similarly, another line plot visualizes inventory levels over time by store, also with markers and solid lines.

Both plots are set to a size of 10x6 inches, and each is titled according to the data metric it represents, helping to clearly differentiate the performance metrics across the two stores.

By embracing data science principles, the retail chain achieved remarkable results. They reduced excess inventory, minimized stockouts, and improved overall supply chain efficiency. Armed with data-driven insights, the retailer now makes strategic decisions with confidence, ensuring they stay ahead of the competition in an ever-evolving market landscape. The implementation of sophisticated analytics tools allowed the retailer to predict consumer buying patterns more accurately and adjust their inventory levels accordingly. This proactive approach not only prevented overstocking but also ensured that popular items were readily available, enhancing customer satisfaction and loyalty. Additionally, the retailer was able to identify inefficiencies in their supply chain processes and make necessary adjustments, leading to reduced operational costs and increased profitability. The success of these initiatives has set a benchmark in the retail industry, proving the immense value of integrating data science into business strategy.

IMPLEMENTATION ROADMAP: INTRODUCTION TO DATA SCIENCE AND DECISION MAKING

This implementation roadmap outlines a step-by-step process for applying in practice the data science techniques presented in this chapter.

Roadmap steps

- *Step 1*: Define objectives and identify key data sources.
- *Step 2*: Define data science objectives, data collection and preparation, data analysis and modeling, and interpretation and decision making.
- *Step 3*: Define key concepts, provide examples, and offer resources for further learning.

Step 1: Define Objectives and Identify Key Data Sources

This initial step is essential, as it lays the groundwork by clearly defining the business objectives that data science aims to support. These objectives may include enhancing revenue streams, refining customer experiences, or streamlining operational processes. Concurrently, it is crucial to identify and prioritize the key data sources that are integral to achieving these objectives. This includes tapping into internal databases, leveraging external datasets, and incorporating relevant third-party repositories. Understanding these elements ensures that the data science efforts are aligned with strategic business goals and are focused on extracting actionable insights from the most impactful data sources.

Define Objectives

Clearly define the business objectives that data science will support, such as increasing revenue, improving customer satisfaction, or optimizing operational efficiency. Setting these goals provides a targeted approach for data analysis and ensures that the outcomes are directly aligned with strategic priorities, facilitating more effective decision-making.

Identify Key Data Sources

Identify the key data sources relevant to achieving the defined objectives, including internal databases, external datasets, and third-party sources. This step is crucial for gathering the most relevant and accurate information, ensuring the data collected is robust and comprehensive enough to support effective analysis and insights.

Step 2: Define Data Science Objectives, Data Collection and Preparation, Data Analysis and Modeling, and Interpretation and Decision Making

Step 2 sets clear data science goals such as predicting trends or understanding customer behavior, then gathers and prepares data to ensure it is accurate and useful. Next, analyze the data to find patterns and insights using techniques like regression or clustering, and finally, interpret these findings to make informed decisions.

Define Data Science Objectives

Specify the specific goals and outcomes to be achieved through data science initiatives, such as predictive modeling, customer segmentation, or anomaly detection. This will guide the selection of tools and methods, ensuring that every step of the process contributes directly to the desired end results.

Data Collection and Preparation

Develop a plan for collecting and preprocessing data, ensuring data quality, completeness, and relevance for analysis. This involves choosing the right sources, addressing missing values and outliers, and transforming data into a format suitable for analysis.

Data Analysis and Modeling

Apply data analysis techniques and modeling algorithms to extract insights and patterns from the data, such as regression analysis, clustering, or classification. This step leverages statistical methods and machine learning algorithms to uncover trends, predict outcomes, and provide a deeper understanding of the data.

Interpretation and Decision Making

Interpret the results of data analysis and modeling to derive actionable insights and inform decision-making processes. This involves translating complex results into understandable findings, ensuring stakeholders can make informed decisions based on the data-driven insights provided.

Step 3: Define Key Concepts, Provide Examples, and Offer Resources for Further Learning

Step 3 is all about building your foundation by defining essential data science concepts like machine learning and predictive modeling, illustrating them with real-world examples, and providing resources such as books and online courses for further exploration and understanding.

Define Key Concepts

Define and explain key data science concepts and terminology relevant to the objectives and methodologies being employed, such as machine learning, predictive modeling, and data visualization. Understanding these concepts is crucial for effectively implementing and leveraging data science techniques, ensuring that all team members are on the same page and can contribute meaningfully to discussions and decisions.

Provide Examples

Illustrate key concepts with examples and case studies to enhance understanding and applicability in real-world scenarios. By demonstrating how abstract principles are applied in practical situations, readers can better grasp the potential impacts and applications of data science in their own fields.

Offer Resources for Further Learning

Provide resources such as books, articles, online courses, and tutorials to enable readers to deepen their understanding of key concepts and terminology. Encouraging ongoing education and exploration of new developments in data science enriches professional growth and ensures that individuals are well-equipped to adapt to evolving technologies and methodologies.

By following this implementation roadmap, readers will be guided through the process of applying data science techniques in practice, from understanding the role of data in business strategy to mastering key concepts and terminology essential for effective decision-making. This comprehensive approach ensures a thorough grasp of how to strategically deploy data science resources and insights to achieve business objectives. It covers the initial steps of defining precise goals, sourcing relevant data, and choosing the right tools, to the advanced stages of analyzing results, interpreting outcomes, and making informed decisions. The roadmap also emphasizes the importance of continuous learning and adaptation in the fast-evolving field of data science, providing a foundation not just for immediate project success but for long-term strategic advantage. This will equip readers not only with technical skills but also with a strategic mindset that leverages data science for competitive benefit decision-making.

CONCLUSION

Mastering these key concepts and terminology allows decision-makers to effectively leverage data science to drive informed decision-making and achieve strategic objectives within their organizations. This chapter provides a foundational understanding of the role of data in business strategy, introduces the data science lifecycle, and explores key concepts and terminology essential for navigating the field of data science and decision-making. By embracing data-driven approaches, organizations can gain a competitive edge, innovate with confidence, and adapt to the evolving business landscape. With a robust grasp of data science principles, professionals can unlock valuable insights, optimize operational processes, and enhance their ability to respond to market changes effectively. This knowledge empowers organizations to not only understand their current data but also to foresee future trends, making strategic decisions that are informed by data, not just intuition. Through practical examples and case studies, this chapter demonstrates how integrating data science into business practices leads to improved efficiencies, stronger strategic positioning, and a sustained ability to outperform competitors. This culminates in a strategic advantage that positions organizations to thrive in a data-driven future.

## CHAPTER 2

FOUNDATIONS OF DATA SCIENCE

I n the realm of data science, the journey begins with data collection, the cornerstone upon which all subsequent analyses and insights are built. This chapter explores the intricacies of data collection, examining the diverse sources, acquisition techniques, and quality considerations that underpin this critical phase. Understanding the methods and tools for effective data collection is essential for ensuring the reliability and validity of the data used in analyses. This chapter also examines the ethical considerations and legal regulations surrounding data acquisition, emphasizing the importance of obtaining data responsibly and transparently. By mastering the foundations of data collection, readers will be equipped with the skills necessary to gather high-quality data that serves as the bedrock for successful data science projects. This overview aims to provide a solid foundation for anyone looking to harness the power of data in their decision-making processes.

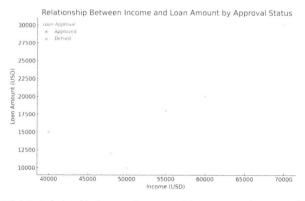

FIGURE 2.1. Relationship between income and loan amount by approval status.

Figure 2.1 depicts the relationship between income and loan amount by approval status. The scatter plot visualizes the relationship between the income levels of customers (in USD) and the corresponding loan amounts requested (in USD). Each point represents an individual customer's loan application, color-coded by the approval status: green for "Approved" and red for "Denied." The plot helps to illustrate patterns or trends in how income may relate to the approval or denial of loan amounts.

From internal databases and Web scraping to sensor networks and social media platforms, understanding the landscape of data sources is essential for ensuring the relevance and reliability of collected data. Moreover, meticulous attention to data quality and integrity is paramount, necessitating validation, cleaning, and preprocessing to rectify errors, inconsistencies, and missing values before analysis can commence.

Once collected, raw data often requires preprocessing to render it amenable to analysis. This chapter navigates through the nuances of data cleaning, transformation, and integration, elucidating best practices and techniques for refining raw data into a cohesive and analyzable format. By addressing errors, standardizing units of measurement, and harmonizing disparate datasets, data scientists pave the way for meaningful insights and discoveries. Subsequently, the chapter examines the realm of exploratory data analysis (EDA), a pivotal step where analysts unravel the hidden patterns, trends, and relationships lurking within the dataset. Through descriptive statistics, data visualization, correlation analysis, and clustering techniques, EDA illuminates the data landscape, empowering analysts to glean insights and formulate hypotheses for further exploration.

As data science unfolds, statistical fundamentals serve as its guiding principles, furnishing the theoretical underpinnings and methodologies for robust data analysis. This chapter explains key statistical concepts such as *probability distributions*, *hypothesis testing*, *regression analysis*, and *statistical inference*, equipping data scientists with the tools to draw meaningful conclusions and make informed decisions.

By mastering the foundations of data collection, preprocessing, exploratory data analysis, and statistical fundamentals, data scientists embark on a transformative journey, unlocking the power of data to drive innovation, inform strategy, and catalyze growth within organizations.

DATA COLLECTION: THE BACKBONE OF DATA SCIENCE

Data collection is the initial step in the data science process, laying the foundation for all subsequent analysis and decision-making. This section explores the key considerations and methodologies involved in collecting data for analysis:

Data Source

Data can be sourced from a variety of sources, including internal databases, external APIs, Web scraping, sensor networks, social media platforms, and third-party data providers. Internal databases might include customer records, sales transactions, or operational logs. External APIs, such as those provided by Google or Twitter, offer access to vast amounts of real-time data. Web scraping involves extracting information from Web sites, while sensor networks gather data from physical environments. Social media platforms provide insights into user behavior and trends, and third-party data providers offer curated datasets. Understanding the availability, reliability, and legality of these data sources is crucial for ensuring the quality and relevance of the collected data.

Data Acquisition Techniques

Different data acquisition techniques may be employed depending on the nature of the data and the desired outcomes. These techniques include manual data entry, where data is inputted by individuals; automated data collection scripts, which use software to gather data without human intervention; data streaming, which captures and processes data in real-time; and real-time data ingestion pipelines, which integrate data from various sources in real-time. Each technique has its advantages and challenges, such as the accuracy and timeliness of manual entry versus the efficiency and scalability of automated methods. Selecting the appropriate technique is vital for effective data collection.

Data Quality and Integrity

Ensuring the quality and integrity of collected data is essential for meaningful analysis and decision-making. This involves validating data for accuracy, completeness, consistency, and timeliness. Accuracy ensures the data reflects real-world scenarios correctly. Completeness ensures no critical data is missing. Consistency ensures data is uniform across the dataset, and timeliness ensures data is up-to-date. Addressing any errors or inconsistencies through data cleaning and preprocessing is crucial. This may involve removing duplicates, correcting errors, and standardizing formats. High-quality data forms the foundation for reliable analysis and accurate insights, making data quality management a priority in data science.

DATA PREPROCESSING: CLEANING AND TRANSFORMING RAW DATA

Raw data collected from various sources often requires preprocessing to make it suitable for analysis. This section reviews the preprocessing techniques and best practices:

Data Cleaning

Data cleaning involves identifying and correcting errors, inconsistencies, and missing values in the dataset. This may include tasks such as removing duplicates, which ensures each record in the dataset is unique and does not skew analysis. Imputing missing values involves filling in gaps in data using

methods like mean, median, or mode substitution, or more advanced techniques like multiple imputation or using algorithms to predict missing values.
Correcting typos involves standardizing text entries to maintain consistency,
which is critical for accurate analysis. Handling outliers is essential to ensure
that extreme values do not distort analytical results, which can be done through
techniques such as capping or transforming data.

Data Transformation

Data transformation involves converting raw data into a more suitable
format for analysis. This may include standardizing units of measurement to
ensure that all data points are comparable, such as converting all weights to
kilograms or lengths to meters. Encoding categorical variables is necessary
for machine learning algorithms, which may involve converting text labels
into numerical values using techniques like one-hot encoding or label encoding. Scaling numerical features ensures that data points are within a similar
range, which can be crucial for algorithms sensitive to the scale of data, such as
normalization or standardization. Performing dimensionality reduction techniques, such as principal component analysis (PCA) or feature selection, helps
simplify the dataset by reducing the number of variables while retaining essential information.

Data Integration

Data integration involves combining data from multiple sources to create
a unified dataset for analysis. This may involve resolving inconsistencies in
data formats, such as converting date formats to a standard structure or aligning numerical scales. Aligning data schemas involves ensuring that data fields
from various sources correspond to one another correctly, which may require
mapping fields from one dataset to fields in another. Merging datasets based
on common identifiers or key variables ensures that the combined dataset is
coherent and comprehensive. Effective data integration is crucial for creating
a holistic view of the data, enabling more accurate and insightful analysis.

UNVEILING INSIGHTS THROUGH EXPLORATORY DATA ANALYSIS

Exploratory Data Analysis (EDA) is a critical step in the data science process, enabling analysts to gain insights into the underlying patterns, trends,
and relationships within the dataset. This section explores the techniques and
methodologies involved in EDA.

Descriptive Statistics

Descriptive statistics provide a summary of the key characteristics of the
dataset, including measures of central tendency (e.g., mean, median), which
give insights into the typical values within the data. Measures of dispersion
(e.g., variance, standard deviation) help understand the spread and variability of the data points. Distributional properties of the data can be explored

through visual tools such as histograms, which display the frequency distribution of data, and box plots, which show the spread and skewness of the data, highlighting outliers and the interquartile range. These statistics form the foundational step in understanding the basic features and quality of the dataset before deeper analysis.

Data Visualization

Data visualization techniques such as scatter plots, histograms, bar charts, and heatmaps are powerful tools for visually exploring and understanding the structure and patterns within the data. Scatter plots help identify relationships and trends between two numerical variables, while histograms provide a visual representation of the distribution of a single variable. Bar charts are useful for comparing categorical data, and heatmaps are effective in showing the magnitude of values across two dimensions, often used to visualize correlation matrices. These visualizations facilitate quick insights into data, making it easier to spot trends, outliers, clusters, and correlations that may not be apparent from raw data alone.

Correlation Analysis

Correlation analysis is used to quantify the strength and direction of relationships between variables in the dataset. The Pearson correlation coefficient measures linear relationships between continuous variables, indicating how changes in one variable are associated with changes in another. The Spearman rank correlation coefficient assesses monotonic relationships, whether linear or non-linear, and is suitable for ordinal data. The rank correlation coefficient of Kendall Tau measures the ordinal association between two measured quantities, providing insights into the rank correlation. These correlation measures are crucial for identifying and understanding the interdependencies among variables, which can inform feature selection and model building in predictive analytics.

Clustering and Dimensionality Reduction

Clustering techniques such as k-means clustering and hierarchical clustering are used to identify natural groupings or clusters within the data. K-means clustering partitions the data into a predefined number of clusters based on similarity, while hierarchical clustering builds a tree of clusters based on the nested grouping of data points. Dimensionality reduction techniques such as principal component analysis (PCA) and t-distributed stochastic neighbor embedding (t-SNE) help visualize high-dimensional data in lower-dimensional space while preserving its structure and relationships. PCA reduces dimensionality by transforming data into principal components that capture the most variance, and t-SNE is used for visualizing complex, high-dimensional data in a way that reveals clusters and patterns. These techniques are essential for simplifying data, reducing noise, and making high-dimensional data more interpretable.

STATISTICAL FUNDAMENTALS FOR DATA ANALYSIS

Statistical fundamentals form the backbone of data analysis, providing the theoretical framework and methodologies for drawing meaningful conclusions from data. This section covers key statistical concepts and techniques essential for data analysis:

Probability Distributions

Probability distributions such as the normal distribution, binomial distribution, and Poisson distribution describe the likelihood of different outcomes in a random experiment. The normal distribution, also known as the bell curve, is crucial for many statistical methods and represents data that clusters around a mean. The binomial distribution models the number of successes in a fixed number of binary (yes/no) trials, such as flipping a coin. The Poisson distribution, on the other hand, is used for modeling the number of events occurring within a fixed interval of time or space, such as the number of emails received per hour. Understanding these distributions is essential for modeling uncertainty, conducting inferential statistics, and making probabilistic predictions in various fields such as finance, healthcare, and engineering.

Hypothesis Testing

Hypothesis testing is a statistical method used to determine whether observed differences or relationships in the data are statistically significant or simply due to chance. It starts with formulating a null hypothesis (no effect or difference) and an alternative hypothesis (an effect or difference exists). Common hypothesis tests include t-tests, which compare the means of two groups; chi-square tests, which assess the association between categorical variables; ANOVA (Analysis of Variance), which compares the means of three or more groups; and correlation tests, which measure the strength and direction of relationships between variables. Hypothesis testing helps researchers validate their assumptions and draw reliable conclusions from sample data, thereby supporting evidence-based decision-making.

Regression Analysis

Regression analysis is a statistical technique used to model the relationship between a dependent variable and one or more independent variables. Linear regression predicts a continuous outcome based on one or more predictors by fitting a straight line to the data. Logistic regression, suitable for binary outcomes, estimates the probability of an event occurring, such as success/failure. Polynomial regression, an extension of linear regression, models nonlinear relationships by fitting a polynomial equation to the data. These regression models are widely used for predictive modeling, trend analysis, and forecasting in various domains, including economics, medicine, and the social sciences, enabling researchers to understand the influence of multiple factors on a target variable.

Statistical Inference

Statistical inference involves drawing conclusions or making predictions about a population based on sample data. Point estimation provides single-value estimates of population parameters, such as the mean or proportion. Interval estimation, like confidence intervals, offers a range of values within which the parameter is expected to lie, providing a measure of uncertainty. Hypothesis testing, a core component of statistical inference, evaluates the validity of assumptions about population parameters based on sample data. Techniques like these are fundamental for making data-driven decisions, conducting scientific research, and formulating policies, as they allow for generalizing findings from samples to broader populations while accounting for variability and uncertainty.

USING ANALYTICS: DATA SCIENCE FOUNDATIONS

This section illuminates the use of analytics and data science foundations, highlighting their efficacy in addressing complex challenges and driving informed decision-making, including:

Data Quality Assurance

Utilize analytics techniques during data collection and preprocessing to ensure data quality and integrity. By performing data validation, cleansing, and transformation, organizations can identify and address issues such as missing values, outliers, and inconsistencies, ensuring the reliability of data for subsequent analysis. For example, data validation rules can be applied to check for logical consistency, such as ensuring that dates are within a plausible range or that numerical values fall within expected limits. Data cleansing processes can then correct or remove erroneous entries, and transformation steps, such as normalizing or standardizing data, can make datasets more uniform and ready for analysis. By ensuring data quality from the outset, organizations enhance the accuracy and trustworthiness of their analytical insights.

Pattern Recognition

Leverage analytics for exploratory data analysis to uncover patterns, trends, and relationships within datasets. By visualizing data using techniques such as histograms, scatter plots, and correlation matrices, analysts can gain insights into underlying structures and distributions, informing further analysis and decision-making processes. For instance, histograms can reveal the distribution of a single variable, showing whether it is normally distributed or skewed. Scatter plots can identify potential correlations between two variables, while correlation matrices can provide a comprehensive view of relationships among multiple variables. These visualizations help analysts quickly grasp the characteristics of the data and identify areas for deeper investigation, driving more informed and targeted analysis.

Inference and Prediction

Apply statistical fundamentals for data analysis to infer relationships and make predictions based on data patterns. By employing techniques such as regression analysis, hypothesis testing, and probability distributions, organizations can derive actionable insights and forecast future outcomes, guiding strategic decision-making and risk management initiatives. Regression analysis, for example, can model the relationship between sales and marketing spend, providing insights into how changes in marketing investment might impact revenue. Hypothesis testing can evaluate the effectiveness of a new product feature by comparing user engagement before and after its introduction. Probability distributions can help in assessing the likelihood of various risk scenarios, aiding in the development of mitigation strategies. These statistical methods enable organizations to make data-driven decisions that are both informed and predictive, enhancing their ability to plan and manage uncertainty effectively.

CASE STUDY: PREDICTIVE MAINTENANCE IN MANUFACTURING

In the realm of manufacturing, downtime due to equipment failure can result in significant losses. Let us explore how *a leading manufacturing company* utilized the foundations of data science to implement predictive maintenance strategies, ensuring optimal equipment performance and minimizing disruptions.

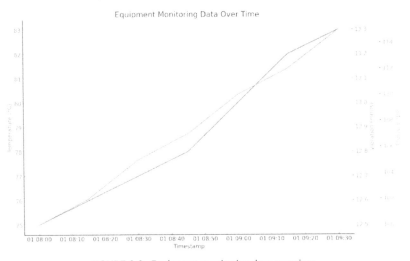

FIGURE 2.2. Equipment monitoring data over time.

Figure 2.2 is a line chart showing how temperature, vibration, and pressure change over time for the equipment. You can observe the trends in these parameters as they lead up to the failure events.

Objective

A *leading manufacturing company* recognized the importance of collecting and preprocessing data from their manufacturing equipment to identify patterns indicative of potential failures. They installed sensors on critical machinery to capture real-time data on factors such as temperature, vibration, and pressure. This data was then aggregated and cleaned to remove noise and inconsistencies, ensuring accuracy in subsequent analyses.

TABLE 2.1. Manufacturing equipment data.

Timestamp	Equipment ID	Temperature (°C)	Vibration (mm/s)	Pressure (psi)	Failure (0: No, 1: Yes)
4/1/24 8:00 AM	EQ001	75	12.5	100	0
4/1/24 8:15 AM	EQ001	76	12.6	102	0
4/1/24 8:30 AM	EQ001	77	12.7	105	0
4/1/24 8:45 AM	EQ001	78	12.8	107	0
4/1/24 9:00 AM	EQ001	80	13.0	110	0
4/1/24 9:15 AM	EQ001	82	13.2	112	1
4/1/24 9:30 AM	EQ001	83	13.3	115	1

Approach

With a vast amount of sensor data at their disposal, *a leading manufacturing company* embarked on exploratory data analysis (EDA) to gain insights into the behavior of their equipment. They visualized the data using techniques such as scatter plots, histograms, and box plots to identify trends, outliers, and correlations. Through EDA, they discovered that certain patterns in sensor readings preceded equipment failures, laying the groundwork for predictive maintenance models.

Result

Armed with a deeper understanding of their data, *the manufacturing company* applied statistical fundamentals to analyze and interpret the patterns uncovered during EDA. They employed techniques such as regression analysis to model the relationship between sensor readings and equipment failures, enabling them to predict when maintenance was required proactively.

This dataset includes:

- *Timestamp:* Date and time when sensor data was recorded.
- *Equipment ID:* A unique identifier for each piece of manufacturing equipment.
- *Temperature (°C):* Temperature readings from sensors installed on the equipment.
- *Vibration (mm/s):* Vibration measurements collected by sensors.
- *Pressure (psi):* Pressure data recorded by sensors.
- *Failure (0: No, 1: Yes):* A binary indicator of whether equipment failure occurred after the corresponding data was recorded.

Example Visualizations

Time Series of Temperature, Vibration, and Pressure

This combined line plot (*Figure 2.3*) shows the variations in temperature, vibration, and pressure over time. It helps to visually assess trends and spot any significant changes that might be related to equipment failures.

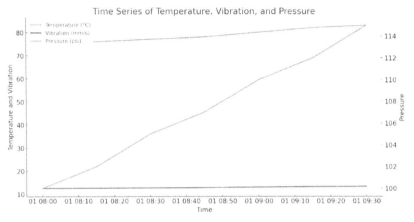

FIGURE 2.3. Time series of temperature, vibration, and pressure.

Correlation Matrix of Temperature, Vibration, Pressure, and Failure

The heatmap (*Figure 2.4*) provides insights into the relationships among temperature, vibration, pressure, and failure events. This visualization can help identify which metrics are most strongly correlated with failures.

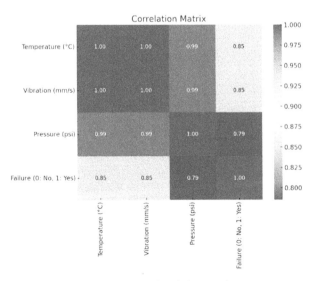

FIGURE 2.4. Correlation matrix.

Failure Events Over Time

This plot (*Figure 2.5*) overlays failure events marked in red on the trends of temperature, vibration, and pressure. It is designed to help pinpoint the conditions under which failures occur and how they relate to changes in operational metrics.

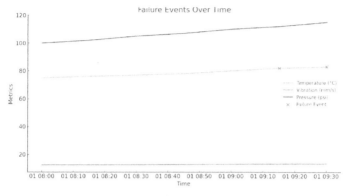

FIGURE 2.5. Failure events over time.

Python code

```python
import pandas as pd
import seaborn as sns
import matplotlib.pyplot as plt

# Data setup
data_2 = {
"Timestamp": ["8:00 AM", "8:15 AM", "8:30 AM", "8:45 AM", "9:00 AM", "9:15 AM", "9:30 AM"],
"Temperature (°C)": [75, 76, 77, 78, 80, 82, 83],
"Vibration (mm/s)": [12.5, 12.6, 12.7, 12.8, 13.0, 13.2, 13.3],
"Pressure (psi)": [100, 102, 105, 107, 110, 112, 115],
"Failure": [0, 0, 0, 0, 0, 1, 1]
}

df_2 = pd.DataFrame(data_2)

# Visualization: Temperature, Vibration, Pressure Trends
plt.figure(figsize=(12, 7))
sns.lineplot(data=df_2, x='Timestamp', y='Temperature (°C)', label='Temperature (°C)', color='red')
sns.lineplot(data=df_2, x='Timestamp', y='Vibration (mm/s)', label='Vibration (mm/s)', color='blue')
sns.lineplot(data=df_2, x='Timestamp', y='Pressure (psi)', label='Pressure (psi)', color='green')
plt.title('Equipment Monitoring: Temp, Vibration, and Pressure')
plt.legend()
plt.show()
```

FIGURE 2.6. An example of Python code.

This Python script is designed for visualizing trends in equipment monitoring data using the "Pandas™," "Seaborn™," and "Matplotlib™" libraries:

- *Data Setup*: The script organizes monitoring data, including timestamps, temperature, vibration, and pressure readings, along with failure indicators, into a dictionary. This dictionary is then converted into a pandas DataFrame for easier handling and visualization.
- *Visualization*: A single plot is created to display trends over time for temperature (in °C), vibration (in mm/s), and pressure (in psi). Each metric is plotted as a separate line on the graph:
  - Temperature is represented in red
  - Vibration in blue
  - Pressure in green

NOTE *To view full color version of all images this text, please visit the companion site for this title.)*

The plot is sized at 12×7 inches to ensure clarity and includes a legend to differentiate between the metrics. The title "Equipment Monitoring: Temp, Vibration, and Pressure" provides a clear description of the plot's focus. This visualization helps in monitoring equipment performance and identifying potential correlations or trends that may lead to failures.

IMPLEMENTATION ROADMAP: FOUNDATIONS OF DATA SCIENCE

This implementation roadmap outlines a step-by-step process for practically applying the data science techniques presented in this chapter. It serves as a guide, offering detailed instructions on each phase of the data science lifecycle, from data collection to analysis and interpretation. The roadmap begins with identifying relevant data sources and implementing effective data acquisition techniques to ensure comprehensive data gathering. Next, it covers data cleaning and preprocessing steps to ensure data quality and integrity. It then delves into various data analysis methods, including exploratory data analysis, pattern recognition, and statistical inference, providing practical tips for uncovering insights and making predictions. Finally, the roadmap addresses how to effectively communicate these insights through visualization and reporting, ensuring that the findings can be leveraged to drive informed decision-making and strategic actions within the organization. This structured approach ensures that all key aspects of data science are covered, enabling practitioners to implement data-driven strategies effectively.

Roadmap steps:
- *Step 1*: Define the data collection strategy, establish the data preprocessing pipeline, and select tools and technologies.
- *Step 2*: Define analysis objectives, conduct data visualization, and perform descriptive statistics.
- *Step 3*: Define statistical techniques, apply statistical methods, and interpret results.

Step 1: Define the Data Collection Strategy, Establish the Data Preprocessing Pipeline, and Select Tools and Technologies

Step 1 lays the groundwork for your data science journey by helping you decide where and how to gather data, set up a system to clean and organize it, and choose the right tools, like Python libraries, to make the process smooth and efficient.

Define Data Collection Strategy

Determine the data sources and methods for collecting relevant data, considering factors such as data availability, quality, and privacy. This involves identifying internal and external data sources, assessing the reliability and accuracy of these sources, and ensuring compliance with data privacy regulations. The strategy should outline the specific data required, the frequency of data collection, and the tools or technologies needed to capture the data. Additionally, it should include plans for data storage, access control, and ensuring that collected data is relevant and aligned with the goals and objectives of the organization.

Establish Data Preprocessing Pipeline

Develop a comprehensive pipeline for preprocessing the collected data, including essential tasks such as data cleaning, normalization, managing missing values, and feature engineering. Data cleaning involves removing duplicates, correcting errors, and ensuring consistency in data formats. Normalization adjusts the data to a common scale without distorting differences in the ranges of values. Managing missing values involves techniques such as imputation or the removal of incomplete records. Feature engineering transforms raw data into meaningful features that enhance model performance. This pipeline ensures that the data is of high quality and ready for analysis, enabling accurate and reliable insights.

Select Tools and Technologies

Choose appropriate tools and technologies for data collection and preprocessing, ensuring they meet the requirements of your data strategy. Python libraries like Pandas and NumPy™ are essential for data manipulation and analysis, offering powerful functions for handling structured data. Additionally, consider data preprocessing platforms and software that provide robust solutions for data integration, cleaning, and transformation. Evaluate tools based on their scalability, ease of use, and compatibility with existing systems. Selecting the right technologies is crucial for efficient data processing and ensures that the data is prepared effectively for subsequent analysis and modeling stages.

Step 2: Define Analysis Objectives, Conduct Data Visualization, and Perform Descriptive Statistics

Step 2 focuses on refining analysis goals, employing visual aids like histograms and scatter plots to unearth patterns, and utilizing descriptive statistics such as mean and median to provide a comprehensive overview of the dataset's traits.

Define Analysis Objectives

Clarify the objectives of exploratory data analysis (EDA) by determining what specific insights you aim to uncover. This could involve identifying patterns and trends within the data, detecting outliers or anomalies, understanding relationships between variables, or assessing the distribution and spread of the data. Clearly defined objectives guide the EDA process, ensuring that the analysis remains focused and relevant to the business goals. Documenting these objectives helps in setting expectations and provides a framework for evaluating the success of the EDA phase.

Conduct Data Visualization

Use data visualization techniques to explore the dataset visually and gain intuitive insights. Create various visual representations, such as histograms to understand the distribution of individual variables, scatter plots to examine relationships between pairs of variables, box plots to identify the presence of outliers and understand data dispersion, and heatmaps to visualize correlations between multiple variables. These visual tools help in quickly identifying patterns, trends, and anomalies, making the data more accessible and easier to interpret. Effective data visualization aids in communicating findings to stakeholders clearly and concisely.

Perform Descriptive Statistics

Calculate descriptive statistics to summarize and describe the major features of the dataset. Compute measures of central tendency, such as the mean, median, and mode, to understand the typical values in the data. Assess measures of dispersion, including standard deviation, variance, and interquartile range, to gauge the spread and variability of the data. Additionally, evaluate the shape of the data distribution using skewness and kurtosis. Descriptive statistics provide a foundational understanding of the dataset, offering essential insights into its structure and characteristics and guiding further analysis and modeling efforts.

Step 3: Define Statistical Techniques, Apply Statistical Methods, and Interpret Results

Step 3 focuses on harnessing statistical tools to uncover insights from the data. By defining statistical techniques like hypothesis testing and regression analysis, applying methods such as correlation analysis and ANOVA, and interpreting the results, it unlocks valuable insights essential for informed decision-making.

Define Statistical Techniques

Identify relevant statistical techniques for data analysis based on the specific objectives and nature of the dataset. Techniques such as hypothesis testing help determine if there are significant differences or effects within the data, while regression analysis models relationships between dependent and independent variables. Analysis of Variance (ANOVA) is useful for comparing means across multiple groups. Other techniques might include time series analysis for temporal data, cluster analysis for grouping similar data points, or survival analysis for event occurrence over time. Selecting the appropriate statistical techniques ensures the analysis is rigorous and aligns with the research or business questions being addressed.

Apply Statistical Methods

Apply statistical methods to analyze relationships and patterns in the data. For correlation analysis, compute correlation coefficients to measure the strength and direction of relationships between variables. Regression modeling, such as linear regression, logistic regression, or polynomial regression, helps predict outcomes and understand the impact of predictor variables. Hypothesis testing, including t-tests, chi-square tests, and ANOVA, assesses whether observed patterns are statistically significant. Implementing these methods involves using statistical software or programming languages like R, Python, or SPSS to perform calculations, generate outputs, and visualize results. Proper application of statistical methods provides robust insights into the data.

Interpret Results

Interpret the results of statistical analyses to draw meaningful insights and make informed decisions based on the data. This involves understanding the statistical significance, confidence intervals, and practical implications of the findings. For example, a significant regression coefficient indicates a meaningful relationship between variables, while a high correlation coefficient suggests a strong association. Contextualize the results within the scope of the research questions or business objectives, considering limitations and potential biases. Communicate the findings effectively to stakeholders through reports, presentations, and visualizations, highlighting key insights and actionable recommendations derived from the data analysis.

By following this implementation roadmap, readers will be equipped with the necessary skills and tools to collect, preprocess, explore, and analyze data effectively. This guide ensures that readers can confidently manage data from initial collection through insightful analysis. The roadmap provides step-by-step instructions, practical tips, and best practices, helping readers build a solid foundation for data science work. By mastering these essential techniques, readers will be well-prepared to drive data-driven decision-making processes, contribute to their organizations' strategic objectives, and tackle more advanced data science challenges with confidence and proficiency.

CONCLUSION

Data scientists can effectively extract actionable insights from data and drive informed decision-making within organizations by mastering the foundations of data collection, preprocessing, exploratory data analysis, and statistical fundamentals. A solid grasp of these foundational elements enables data scientists to manage diverse datasets, ensuring their accuracy, consistency, and relevance. They can uncover hidden patterns, trends, and correlations that inform strategic initiatives by skillfully employing data visualization techniques. Moreover, a deep understanding of statistical methods allows them to rigorously analyze data, validate hypotheses, and make reliable predictions.

Consequently, data scientists equipped with these essential skills are better positioned to contribute to the success of their organization, fostering innovation, optimizing processes, and enhancing overall performance through data-driven approaches. Their ability to turn raw data into meaningful insights empowers stakeholders to make evidence-based decisions, ensuring sustained growth and competitive advantage in an increasingly datacentric world.

## CHAPTER 3

DATA VISUALIZATION AND COMMUNICATION

I n the realm of data science, the ability to effectively communicate insights derived from data analysis is paramount. This chapter introduces the principles, tools, and techniques essential for creating impactful visualizations and strategies for communicating data-driven insights to stakeholders. Beginning with an exploration of the fundamental principles of data visualization, clarity, simplicity, accuracy, relevance, and engagement are emphasized as guiding principles for crafting effective visualizations. This chapter also examines the psychological aspects of how humans perceive and interpret visual information, which is crucial for designing visualizations that are not only informative but also intuitive and persuasive. It covers several types of visualizations, from basic charts to complex infographics and interactive dashboards, discussing their specific uses and best practices. Additionally, the chapter addresses the challenges of presenting complex data in ways that are accessible to diverse audiences, ensuring that key messages are conveyed clearly and effectively. By integrating theory with practical application, this chapter equips readers with the skills necessary to transform raw data into compelling visual stories that can influence decision-making and drive business strategies.

Figure 3.1 is a pie chart showing the market share of each product category within the East and West regions. These visualizations allow you to see which products dominate the market in each region.

Moving beyond principles, the myriad tools and techniques available for data visualization are examined. From popular libraries such as Matplotlib™ and Tableau™ to emerging technologies like GIS software and data storytelling, there are a breadth of options for creating static and interactive visualizations. Moreover, effective dashboard design incorporates principles and strategies for leveraging infographics and data storytelling to engage and inform audiences.

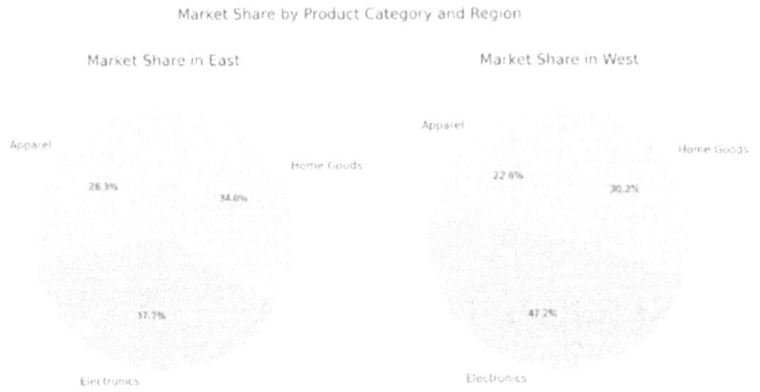

Market Share by Product Category and Region

Market Share in East   Market Share in West

FIGURE 3.1. Market share by product category and region.

The importance of effective data communication strategies should be underscored, emphasizing the need to tailor communication to the audience, tell compelling stories with data, utilize multiple channels for dissemination, solicit feedback, and foster data literacy within organizations. By embracing the principles of data visualization and communication and leveraging appropriate tools and strategies, organizations can unlock the full potential of their data, driving informed decision-making, fostering collaboration, and catalyzing innovation.

PRINCIPLES OF DATA VISUALIZATION

Data visualization is more than just creating aesthetically pleasing charts and graphs; it is about effectively communicating complex information in a clear and concise manner. This section reviews the fundamental principles of data visualization:

Clarity and Simplicity

Visualizations should be clear, concise, and easy to understand. Avoid clutter and unnecessary complexity and focus on conveying the key insights succinctly. Simplifying the presentation helps ensure that the viewer can grasp the intended message without confusion. Strive for minimalism where possible, removing any elements that do not support comprehension of the data. Use direct labels and clean axes to make charts easier to read and interpret. This approach not only improves the viewer's experience but also enhances the overall effectiveness of the communication.

Accuracy and Integrity

Ensure that visualizations accurately represent the underlying data without distorting or misleading information. Use appropriate scales, labels, and annotations to provide context and clarity. It is crucial to maintain the integrity of the data by choosing graph types and scales that reflect the true nature of the data. Misrepresentation can lead not only to misunderstandings but also to decisions that are based on faulty interpretations. Always verify that visual elements such as axes and reference lines are clear and accurately convey the right quantities.

Relevance and Context

Visualizations should be relevant to the audience and the intended message. Provide context and background information to help viewers interpret the data and understand its implications. Tailor your visualizations to the needs and knowledge level of your audience, ensuring that each visualization speaks directly to their concerns and interests. Contextualizing data with appropriate comparisons and benchmarks can significantly enhance the audience"s understanding and make the insights more actionable.

Use of Color and Visual Elements

Choose colors, fonts, and visual elements thoughtfully to enhance readability and comprehension. Use color palettes that are accessible to all viewers and avoid using color for purely decorative purposes. Colors should be used to highlight significant data points and guide the viewer's attention to the most important parts of the visualization. Ensure that there is a good contrast between text and background colors and use fonts that are easy to read even at smaller sizes. The goal is to create a visual appeal that aids in the data storytelling process without compromising the ability of the viewer to quickly understand the information.

Interactivity and Engagement

Interactive visualizations allow viewers to explore data dynamically and gain deeper insights. Incorporate interactive elements such as tooltips, filters, and drill-down capabilities to engage viewers and encourage exploration. This type of engagement not only makes the experience more immersive but also allows users to personalize the exploration of the data, making discoveries that are relevant to their specific interests or concerns. Interactive elements should be intuitive and seamlessly integrated so that they enhance, rather than complicate, the user experience.

TOOLS AND TECHNIQUES FOR DATA VISUALIZATION

A plethora of tools and techniques are available for creating data visualizations, ranging from basic charts and graphs to advanced interactive dashboards. This section explores some popular tools and techniques for data visualization:

Data Visualization Libraries

Python libraries such as Matplotlib, Seaborn™, and Plotly™, and JavaScript libraries like D3.js™ and Highcharts™ are widely used for creating static and interactive visualizations. These tools offer a vast range of capabilities, from simple plots to complex, multi-plot layouts, enabling users to tailor visual presentations to their specific analysis needs. Each library comes with unique functionalities that can be used across various data types and visualization goals. For instance, Plotly provides extensive support for interactive features, making it ideal for Web-based projects, while Matplotlib excels at creating publication-quality figures in a variety of hardcopy formats and interactive environments.

Business Intelligence (BI) Tools

BI platforms such as Tableau, Power BI™, and Qlik Sense™ provide powerful features for creating interactive dashboards, reports, and data visualizations without requiring extensive programming knowledge. These tools facilitate quick insights into data through drag-and-drop interfaces, allowing users to manipulate and experiment with data dynamically. They support decision-making processes by making complex data accessible and understandable through visual analysis. These platforms often include features for data blending, real-time access, and collaborative analytics, making them invaluable in corporate environments where decisions need to be data-driven and timely.

Geographic Information Systems (GIS)

GIS software such as ArcGIS and QGIS enables users to create maps and spatial visualizations to analyze and visualize geographic data. These systems are crucial in fields ranging from urban planning and environmental management to public health and marketing. GIS tools allow for the layering of different data sets on top of geographical maps, providing insights into spatial patterns and relationships. They support a wide range of functionalities, including spatial data analysis, geocoding, routing, and spatial statistics, which are vital for making informed decisions based on geographical information.

Infographics and Data Storytelling

Infographics combine visual elements with concise text to convey complex information in a visually appealing and easy-to-understand format. They are particularly effective for reaching broader audiences by simplifying detailed data into digestible visual pieces that emphasize key points. Data storytelling involves using narratives, anecdotes, and visualizations to tell a compelling story with data. It transforms statistical information into engaging stories that capture attention and convey insights in a way that is both informative and memorable. This method helps bridge the gap between data scientists and non-technical stakeholders by making the data relatable and impactful.

Dashboard Design Principles

Effective dashboard design involves organizing information logically, prioritizing key metrics, and using visual elements such as charts, graphs, and KPIs to convey insights immediately. Dashboards should be intuitive, providing all necessary information immediately with options to drill down for more detailed analysis. A good dashboard design ensures that the most critical data is front and center while also allowing for customization to meet the specific needs of different users. Visual consistency, clear labeling, and strategic use of color enhance the user experience and facilitate faster comprehension of the presented data.

EFFECTIVE DATA COMMUNICATION STRATEGIES

Communicating data-driven insights effectively is essential for driving informed decision-making and fostering collaboration within organizations. This section discusses strategies for effectively communicating data insights:

Know Your Audience

Tailor your communication style and visualizations to the preferences and needs of your audience. Consider their level of expertise, background knowledge, and specific interests when presenting data. This approach ensures that the information is not only accessible but also resonant with the audience, making complex data insights easier to grasp and act upon. Understanding the familiarity of the audience with data visualization techniques can also guide the complexity of the visuals used, ensuring that the presentations are both informative and engaging without being overwhelming.

Tell a Story

Structure your communication around a clear narrative that highlights the key insights, challenges, and implications of the data. Use storytelling techniques to engage your audience and make the data more relatable and memorable. Effective storytelling in data science can transform raw data into a compelling plot that guides the audience through logical conclusions and actionable insights. This method helps in simplifying complex analyses and drawing attention to the most crucial parts of the data, thereby enhancing the impact of the information presented.

Use Multiple Channels

Utilize a variety of communication channels, including presentations, reports, emails, and interactive dashboards, to reach different stakeholders and ensure widespread dissemination of insights. This multi-channel approach helps in accommodating diverse preferences for consuming information and increases the chances that the data insights will reach a broader audience effectively. Each channel can be optimized to suit its format while maintaining consistent messaging across platforms, ensuring coherent and unified communication.

Solicit Feedback

Encourage open dialogue and feedback from stakeholders to ensure that your communication is clear, relevant, and impactful. Use feedback to refine your visualizations and communication strategies over time. This interactive process not only improves the quality of data presentations but also builds trust and engagement among stakeholders. It allows the presenter to adjust aspects of the communication based on direct responses, ensuring the data resonates well with the audience and fulfills its intended purpose.

Foster Data Literacy

Invest in training and education initiatives to enhance data literacy skills among employees and stakeholders. Provide resources, workshops, and first-hand training to empower individuals to interpret, analyze, and communicate data effectively. Boosting data literacy across an organization promotes a more data-driven culture, where stakeholders can make better-informed decisions and contribute more effectively to discussions around data. This investment in education helps demystify data and opens new opportunities for innovation and efficiency within the organization.

USING ANALYTICS: DATA VISUALIZATION AND COMMUNICATION

This section focuses on using analytics for data visualization and communication, highlighting their efficacy in addressing complex challenges and driving informed decision-making, including:

Insights Communication

Utilize data visualization principles and tools to effectively communicate insights derived from analytics. By creating visually compelling charts, graphs, and dashboards, organizations can convey complex information in a clear and intuitive manner, enabling stakeholders to grasp key findings and make informed decisions. Effective insight communication involves not only displaying data but also highlighting trends, patterns, and anomalies that could influence strategic choices. This approach not only improves understanding but also enhances engagement by making the data accessible and actionable. It is crucial to choose the right visualization tools that align with the nature of the data and the message it carries.

Interactive Exploration

Leverage advanced data visualization techniques and tools to facilitate interactive exploration of data. By providing users with dynamic tools and customizable views, organizations can empower stakeholders to explore data from different perspectives, uncovering deeper insights and opportunities for action. This interactive capability allows users to drill down into specifics, adjust parameters, and even simulate scenarios to see potential outcomes. Interactive exploration transforms static data into a vibrant analytical tool, fostering a deeper understanding and initiative-taking engagement with the data and supporting more nuanced and informed decision-making.

Storytelling and Persuasion

Apply effective data communication strategies to tell compelling stories and persuade stakeholders to act based on analytics insights. By framing data within a narrative context, using persuasive language, and incorporating relevant anecdotes and examples, organizations can engage and inspire stakeholders to embrace data-driven decision-making and drive positive change. The art of storytelling in data communication can make complex information more relatable and memorable, effectively mobilizing teams or persuading decision-makers to act. Through well-crafted stories, data not only informs but also motivates, thereby bridging the gap between insights and impact.

CASE STUDY: MARKET TREND ANALYSIS FOR RETAIL EXPANSION

In the competitive landscape of retail, understanding market trends is essential for strategic expansion decisions. This case study highlights how a major market retailer utilized data visualization and communication strategies to analyze market trends effectively and drive informed expansion initiatives. Through detailed analytics, the retailer was able to identify potential growth areas, assess consumer behavior, and predict future market movements, providing a solid foundation for strategic decision-making and expansion planning in various geographic regions.

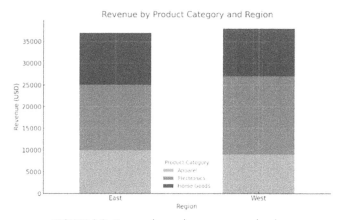

FIGURE 3.2. Revenue by product category and region.

Figure 3.2 is a stacked bar chart showing the revenue distribution by product category for each region. This visualization allows you to see the contribution of each product category to the total revenue in both the East and West regions.

Objective

A major market retailer recognized the importance of conveying complex market data in a clear and intuitive manner. They adhered to principles of data visualization, such as simplicity, clarity, and relevance, to ensure their visualizations effectively communicated key insights. By selecting appropriate chart types, colors, and labels, they aimed to enhance understanding and facilitate decision-making among stakeholders.

Approach

Equipped with a plethora of market data, this *major market retailer* employed innovative tools and techniques for data visualization. They leveraged platforms like Tableau, Power BI, and Matplotlib to create interactive dashboards and visualizations that allowed users to explore market trends dynamically. Using techniques such as heatmaps, trend lines, and geographical mapping, they provided stakeholders with actionable insights into market dynamics and consumer behavior.

Result

Recognizing that effective communication is key to driving action, *the major market retailer implemented* strategies to convey their findings persuasively. They tailored their visualizations to different audience segments, presenting high-level summaries for executives and detailed analyses for operational teams. They also supplemented visualizations with narrative explanations and annotations to provide context and highlight key takeaways effectively.

TABLE 3.1. Market retailer market data.

Date	Region	Product Category	Revenue (USD)	Market Share (%)	Trend
1/1/2024	East	Electronics	15000	20	Growing
1/1/2024	East	Apparel	10000	15	Stable
1/1/2024	East	Home Goods	12000	18	Declining
1/1/2024	West	Electronics	18000	25	Growing
1/1/2024	West	Apparel	9000	12	Stable
1/1/2024	West	Home Goods	11000	16	Declining

This dataset includes:

- *Date*: The date when sales data was recorded.
- *Region*: The geographical region where the sales occurred.
- *Product Category*: The category of the product sold.
- *Sales Revenue (USD)*: The revenue generated from sales of the product category in that region on that date.
- *Market Share (%)*: The percentage of the market share held by the product category in that region on that date.
- *Trend*: The trend of the market for that product category in that region on that date (e.g., growing, stable, and declining).

Sample Visualizations

Revenue by Product Category for Each Region

This grouped bar chart (*Figure 3.3*) displays the revenue generated from electronics, apparel, and home goods in the East and West regions. It clearly illustrates which categories are performing better in each region.

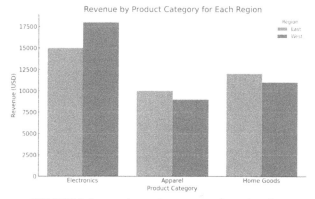

FIGURE 3.3. Revenue by product category for each region.

Market Share by Product Category for Each Region

The bar chart (*Figure 3.4*) shows the market share distribution for each product category within each region. This helps in understanding the competitive positioning of each category in the East and West regions.

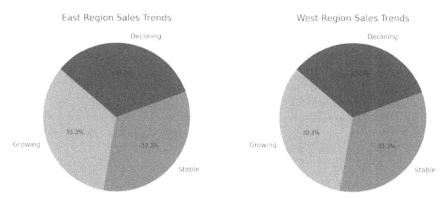

FIGURE 3.4. Market share by product category for each region.

Sales Trends for Product Categories Across Regions

The pie charts (*Figure 3.5*) break down the sales trends (growing, stable, and declining) for each region. This visualization is useful for quickly assessing the market dynamics of different product categories within each region.

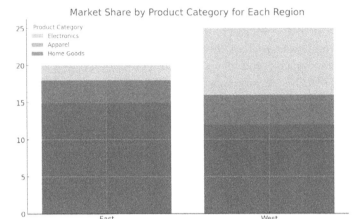

FIGURE 3.5. East and west regions sales trends.

Python code

```
1  import pandas as pd
2  import seaborn as sns
3  import matplotlib.pyplot as plt
4
5  # Data setup
6  data_3 = {
7    "Date": ["1/1/2024", "1/1/2024", "1/1/2024", "1/1/2024", "1/1/2024", "1/1/2024"],
8    "Region": ["East", "East", "East", "West", "West", "West"], "Product Category": ["Electronics", "Apparel", "Home Goods", "Ele
9    "Market Share (%)": [20, 15, 18, 25, 12, 16], "Trend": ["Growing", "Stable", "Declining", "Growing", "Stable", "Declining"]
10  }
11
12  df_3 = pd.DataFrame(data_3)
13
14  # Visualization: Revenue by Product Category and Region
15  plt.figure(figsize=(10, 6))
16  sns.barplot(data=df_3, x='Product Category', y='Revenue (USD)', hue='Region')
17  plt.title('Revenue by Product Category and Region')
18  plt.show()
```

FIGURE 3.6. An example of Python code.

This Python script creates a bar plot to visualize revenue data by product category and region using the "Pandas™," "Seaborn™," and "Matplotlib™" libraries:

- *Data Setup*: It organizes data into a dictionary with fields for date, region, product category, revenue, market share, and trend status. This data is then converted into a pandas DataFrame, making it structured and easy to manipulate for visualization.
- *Visualization*: The script generates a bar plot with the product categories (electronics, apparel, and home goods) on the x-axis and revenue in USD on the y-axis. Assorted colors represent different regions (East and West) to show comparative revenues between these regions for each product category:
  - The plot is sized at 10x6 inches for clear visibility.
  - The title "Revenue by Product Category and Region" succinctly describes what the visualization represents, allowing for quick understanding of the distribution of the data and comparison between different regions and product categories.

This visualization is particularly useful for analyzing regional sales performance across different product lines, helping identify strong and weak sectors within each region. By embracing data visualization and communication strategies, *a major market retailer* gained valuable insights into market trends and consumer behavior, guiding their expansion decisions. Through compelling visualizations and clear communication, they successfully communicated complex market insights to stakeholders, facilitating consensus and alignment on strategic initiatives. As a result, the *major market retailer* achieved sustainable growth and maintained their position as a leader in the retail industry.

IMPLEMENTATION ROADMAP: DATA VISUALIZATION AND COMMUNICATION

This implementation roadmap outlines a step-by-step process for applying in practice the data visualization and communication techniques presented in this chapter. It serves as a practical guide, providing clear instructions on how to effectively collect, analyze, and interpret data to drive informed decision-making within any organization. Through this structured approach, users can learn to harness the power of data visualization tools and strategies to present complex data in a clear and impactful manner, thereby enhancing their ability to communicate key findings and insights to stakeholders and decision-makers across various disciplines.

Roadmap steps:

- *Step 1*: Understand visualization principles, study visual encoding, and explore design best practices.
- *Step 2*: Explore visualization tools, learn visualization techniques, and practice interactive visualization.
- *Step 3*: Understand audience needs, craft compelling narratives, and embrace multimodal communication.

Step 1: Understand Visualization Principles, Study Visual Encoding, and Explore Design Best Practices

Step 1 is your foundation in data visualization, encompassing understanding fundamental principles like clarity and relevance, studying diverse encoding techniques such as color and size, and exploring design strategies including layout and typography to craft compelling and informative visualizations.

Understand Visualization Principles

Familiarize yourself with fundamental principles of data visualization, such as clarity, simplicity, accuracy, and relevance, to ensure that visual representations are both understandable and actionable. Understanding these principles helps in designing visualizations that communicate insights clearly and effectively without overwhelming the viewer.

Study Visual Encoding

Learn about different visual encoding techniques, including position, color, size, shape, and texture, and their applications in conveying data effectively. Understanding how to apply these techniques can significantly enhance the interpretability of data, helping viewers quickly grasp the underlying patterns and relationships.

Explore Design Best Practices

Study design best practices for creating visually appealing and informative visualizations, including considerations such as layout, typography, and use of whitespace. Mastering these elements can improve the readability and impact of your data visualizations, ensuring that they not only capture attention but also convey the intended message succinctly and effectively.

Step 2: Explore Visualization Tools, Learn Visualization Techniques, and Practice Interactive Visualization

Step 2 digs deep into data visualization, guiding you through popular tools like Tableau and Matplotlib, teaching various techniques such as bar charts and heatmaps, and encouraging firsthand practice with interactive features like tooltips and filters to enhance user engagement and data exploration.

Explore Visualization Tools

Familiarize yourself with popular data visualization tools and platforms, such as Tableau, Power BI, Matplotlib, and Seaborn. These tools offer diverse functionalities that cater to different visualization needs and can significantly enhance the ability to communicate complex data stories effectively.

Learn Visualization Techniques

Gain proficiency with various visualization techniques, including bar charts, line charts, scatter plots, histograms, heatmaps, and treemaps, and understand when to use each type of visualization. Knowing the strengths and limitations of each can help in choosing the most effective way to present data for specific analytical needs.

Practice Interactive Visualization

Experiment with interactive visualization techniques to engage users and enable exploration of data insights, such as tooltips, filters, and drill-down capabilities. Interactive elements can transform static data into a dynamic exploration tool, thereby enhancing user understanding and engagement with the data presented.

Step 3: Understand Audience Needs, Craft Compelling Narratives, and Embrace Multimodal Communication

Step 3 focuses on communicating data effectively by understanding the needs of your audience, crafting engaging narratives to captivate them, and embracing a range of communication channels such as reports, presentations, and infographics to deliver insights tailored to different stakeholders.

Understand Audience Needs

Develop compelling narratives around your data insights, using storytelling techniques to engage and captivate your audience. Weave your data into a story that connects with their experiences and challenges, making the abstract data more tangible and impactful.

Craft Compelling Narratives

Develop compelling narratives around your data insights, using storytelling techniques to engage and captivate your audience.

Embrace Multimodal Communication

Explore various communication channels and formats, including reports, presentations, dashboards, and infographics, to effectively communicate data insights to different stakeholders. Utilizing a mix of mediums ensures broader accessibility and comprehension, catering to diverse preferences and enhancing the overall impact of the data shared.

By following this implementation roadmap, readers will gain proficiency in data visualization principles, tools, and techniques, enabling them to create visually compelling and informative visualizations and effectively communicate data insights to diverse audiences. This guidance will empower readers to transform raw data into actionable insights that can inform decision-making processes, enhance strategic planning, and improve outcomes across various domains. By mastering these visualization skills, individuals can better leverage the power of data to support arguments, reveal trends, and make data-driven decisions more accessible and understandable to stakeholders.

CONCLUSION

By adhering to the principles of data visualization, leveraging appropriate tools and techniques, and adopting effective communication strategies, organizations can unlock the full potential of their data and drive meaningful change and innovation. This approach not only enhances internal decision-making processes but also improves external communications with stakeholders, customers, and partners. Effective data visualization and communication foster a data-driven culture that embraces transparency, encourages curiosity, and stimulates continuous improvement. Through engaging and insightful visualizations, organizations can convey complex data in an intuitive format that informs strategic decisions and inspires innovative solutions to challenging problems, leading to enhanced business performance and competitive advantage.

## CHAPTER 4

PREDICTIVE ANALYTICS AND MACHINE LEARNING

Predictive analytics and machine learning represent the forefront of data science, offering powerful tools to extract insights and make informed predictions about future outcomes. This chapter serves as a guide to the fundamentals of predictive modeling, supervised and unsupervised learning techniques, and best practices for model evaluation and validation. It delves into the methodologies that enable machines to learn from data, adapt to new findings, and identify patterns that are crucial for making accurate predictions. Readers will learn how to harness these techniques to solve practical problems across various industries, improve decision-making processes, and optimize strategic outcomes.

Figure 4.1 is a time series plot showing the total sales per day based on the dataset provided. This visualization helps you see the revenue fluctuations over the two days recorded in the dataset.

The outset embarks on an exploration of predictive modeling, delineating the step-by-step process from problem formulation to model deployment. By articulating clear business objectives, preparing data meticulously, selecting appropriate models, and evaluating performance rigorously, organizations lay the groundwork for effective predictive analytics initiatives.

Exploring deeper, it is possible to navigate through the landscape of supervised and unsupervised learning techniques, elucidating the distinctions between these methodologies and their respective applications. In supervised learning, models are trained on labeled data to predict outcomes, while unsupervised learning uncovers hidden patterns within unlabeled data. Through regression and classification in supervised learning and clustering and dimensionality reduction in unsupervised learning, organizations gain the tools to uncover insights and drive decision-making.

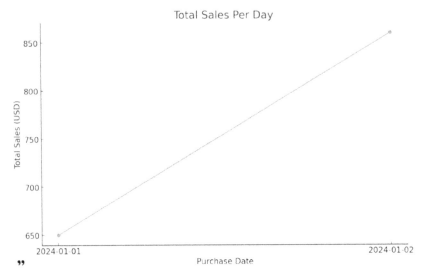

FIGURE 4.1. Total sales per day.

It is crucial to examine the nuances of model evaluation and validation, emphasizing the importance of selecting appropriate performance metrics, employing cross-validation techniques, and guarding against overfitting and underfitting. By mastering these principles and practices, organizations can harness the full potential of predictive analytics and machine learning to extract valuable insights from data, drive informed decision-making, and stay ahead in today's data-driven landscape.

INTRODUCTION TO PREDICTIVE MODELING

Predictive modeling involves using historical data and statistical algorithms to forecast future outcomes or trends. This section provides an overview of the predictive modeling process.

Problem Formulation

Define the predictive modeling problem, including the target variable to be predicted and the available features or predictors. Clearly articulate the business objectives and desired outcomes of the modeling exercise. This step is crucial for aligning the model with organizational goals and ensuring that the effort focuses on relevant predictions that can significantly impact decision-making processes.

Data Preparation

Prepare the data for modeling by cleaning, preprocessing, and transforming the raw data into a suitable format. This may involve tasks such as data cleaning, feature engineering, and normalization. Proper data preparation enhances the quality of the input, which is critical for developing reliable and effective models, thereby increasing the chances of achieving accurate predictions.

Model Selection

Select appropriate machine learning algorithms or statistical models based on the nature of the problem, the type of data, and the desired outcomes. Consider factors such as interpretability, scalability, and computational efficiency when choosing models. The selection of the right model is pivotal as it can influence the effectiveness of the predictive outcomes, ensuring that the model fits well with the complexity and nuances of the data.

Model Training

Train the selected models using historical data, splitting the dataset into training and validation sets to assess model performance. Adjust model parameters and hyperparameters as needed to optimize performance. This phase involves iterative adjustments and testing to fine-tune the model for the best possible outcomes on unseen data, ensuring robustness and reliability.

Model Evaluation

Evaluate the trained models using appropriate metrics to assess their predictive accuracy, generalization capabilities, and robustness. Compare multiple models and select the best-performing model for deployment. This critical step ensures that the model chosen not only performs well on historical data but is also capable of delivering reliable predictions in real-world scenarios.

Model Deployment

Deploy the trained model into production environments, integrating it with existing systems and processes to generate real-time predictions or recommendations. Monitor model performance over time and update as needed to maintain accuracy and effectiveness. Deployment involves not only the integration of the model into business processes but also continuous monitoring and maintenance to adapt to new data or changes in external conditions, ensuring sustained performance.

SUPERVISED AND UNSUPERVISED LEARNING TECHNIQUES

Supervised and unsupervised learning are two primary categories of machine learning techniques, each serving different purposes and use cases. This section explores the differences between supervised and unsupervised learning and common techniques within each category:

Supervised Learning

In supervised learning, the model is trained on labeled data, where each data point is associated with a known outcome or target variable. This approach is foundational in scenarios where the relationship between input variables and a desired output is clear and defined. Common supervised learning techniques include:

Regression

Regression models are used to predict a continuous target variable based on one or more input features. Examples include linear regression, polynomial regression, and support vector regression. These models are integral in fields such as economics for predicting prices, finance for forecasting market trends, and healthcare for estimating patient outcomes.

Classification

Classification models are used to predict a categorical target variable or class label based on input features. Examples include logistic regression, decision trees, random forests, and support vector machines. These models are widely applied in email filtering for spam detection, image recognition for categorizing objects, and customer segmentation for marketing strategies.

Unsupervised Learning

In unsupervised learning, the model is trained on unlabeled data, where the goal is to uncover hidden patterns or structures within the data. This type of learning is pivotal in discovering the intrinsic grouping or distribution of data without prior labels. Common unsupervised learning techniques include:

Clustering

Clustering algorithms group similar data points together into clusters based on their features or attributes. Examples include k-means clustering, hierarchical clustering, and DBSCAN. These techniques are essential in market research for identifying distinct customer segments, genetic research for classifying similar genetic profiles, and document management for organizing large sets of text data.

Dimensionality Reduction

Dimensionality reduction techniques reduce the number of features in the dataset while preserving its structure and variance. Examples include principal component analysis (PCA), t-distributed stochastic neighbor embedding (t-SNE), and autoencoders. These methods are crucial for simplifying complex data, enhancing visualizations, and improving the efficiency of other machine learning algorithms.

MODEL EVALUATION AND VALIDATION

Model evaluation and validation are critical steps in the predictive modeling process to ensure that models generalize well to unseen data and perform effectively in real-world scenarios. This section discusses best practices for model evaluation and validation.

Performance Metrics

Select appropriate performance metrics to evaluate the model's performance based on the specific problem and objectives. Common metrics for regression include mean squared error (MSE), root mean squared error (RMSE), and R-squared (R^2). These metrics help assess the variance and bias in predictions, which are crucial for financial forecasting and energy consumption estimation. For classification, common metrics include accuracy, precision, recall, F1-score, and area under the receiver operating characteristic (ROC) curve. These metrics are vital for applications such as disease diagnosis, customer churn prediction, and image classification, where the balance between several types of errors is critical.

Cross-Validation

Use cross-validation techniques such as k-fold cross-validation or stratified cross-validation to assess model performance on multiple subsets of the data. This method is essential for avoiding biased estimates of model performance and ensuring robustness, particularly in applications like credit scoring or sentiment analysis where the dataset may not be uniformly distributed across categories.

Model Selection

Compare multiple models using cross-validation and performance metrics to select the best-performing model for deployment. Consider factors such as predictive accuracy, interpretability, and computational efficiency when choosing models. This stage is critical in sectors like marketing and risk management, where deploying the optimal model can significantly impact the bottom line.

Validation Strategies

Validate the trained model using holdout validation, where the dataset is split into training and validation sets or using techniques such as bootstrapping or Monte Carlo simulation for more robust validation. These strategies are crucial in scenarios where models must perform well under varying market conditions or consumer behaviors.

Overfitting and Underfitting

Be mindful of overfitting, where the model learns to memorize the training data but fails to generalize to unseen data, and underfitting, where the model is too simple to capture the underlying patterns in the data. Use regularization techniques, feature selection, and model tuning to mitigate overfitting and underfitting. Adjusting these parameters is essential for achieving the best trade-off between model complexity and predictive performance, particularly in complex domains like autonomous driving or algorithmic trading, where precise model tuning can influence performance and safety.

USING ANALYTICS: PREDICTIVE ANALYTICS AND MACHINE LEARNING

This section illuminates the use of predictive analytics and machine learning, highlighting their efficacy in addressing complex challenges and driving informed decision-making, including:

Predictive Modeling

Employ predictive analytics techniques to develop models that forecast future outcomes based on historical data. By applying supervised learning algorithms such as regression and classification, organizations can build predictive models to anticipate trends, identify patterns, and make informed decisions about future actions and strategies. This approach is especially valuable in industries such as finance, healthcare, and retail, where understanding future consumer behavior, market conditions, or health outcomes can significantly influence business practices and policy decisions.

Unsupervised Learning

Leverage unsupervised learning techniques to uncover hidden patterns and structures within data without the need for labeled outcomes. By using clustering algorithms and dimensionality reduction techniques, organizations can segment data into meaningful groups, identify anomalies, and gain insights into underlying data distributions, guiding exploratory analysis and decision-making processes. This method is critical in areas like customer segmentation, fraud detection, and market research, where the insights derived from unsupervised learning can inform marketing strategies, operational adjustments, and product development initiatives.

Model Evaluation and Validation

Implement robust model evaluation and validation processes to assess the performance and reliability of predictive models. By employing techniques such as cross-validation, confusion matrices, and performance metrics like accuracy, precision, recall, and F1-score, organizations can validate model accuracy and generalization ability, ensuring that models are robust and dependable for real-world applications. Thorough evaluation and validation are crucial in sectors such as autonomous driving and medical diagnostics, where the accuracy and reliability of models can directly impact safety and patient outcomes.

CASE STUDY: PERSONALIZED RECOMMENDATIONS IN E-COMMERCE

In the dynamic world of e-commerce, providing personalized recommendations to customers is crucial for enhancing the user experience and driving sales. By understanding individual customer preferences and behaviors, businesses can offer more relevant products, improving satisfaction and loyalty.

Let us explore how a leading online retailer leveraged predictive analytics and machine learning techniques to deliver tailored product recommendations, thereby increasing customer engagement and revenue. This case study examines the methodologies used, the data harnessed, and the impact of personalized recommendations on overall business performance and customer retention rates.

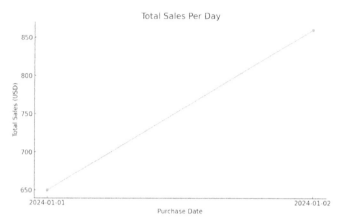

FIGURE 4.2. Total sales per day.

Figure 4.2 is a time series plot showing the total sales per day. This visualization helps you see the revenue fluctuations over the two days recorded in the dataset.

Objective

A *leading online retailer* embarked on a journey to harness the power of predictive modeling to understand customer preferences and behavior. They recognized that historical transaction data contained valuable insights that could be used to predict future purchasing patterns. By employing predictive modeling techniques, they aimed to anticipate customer needs and offer relevant product recommendations in real-time.

TABLE 4.1. Online retailer predictive modeling data.

Customer ID	Product ID	Category	Price (USD)	Purchase Date
001	ABC123	Electronics	500	2024-01-01
002	XYZ456	Apparel	50	2024-01-01
003	LMN789	Home Goods	100	2024-01-01
004	ABC123	Electronics	500	2024-01-02
005	PQR789	Electronics	300	2024-01-02
006	XYZ456	Apparel	60	2024-01-02

Approach

A *leading online retailer* explored both supervised and unsupervised learning techniques to uncover patterns and relationships within their data. They utilized supervised learning algorithms, such as logistic regression and random forests, to predict customer preferences based on past behavior. Additionally, they employed unsupervised learning techniques, such as clustering and association rule mining, to identify hidden patterns and group comparable products for recommendation purposes.

Result

To ensure the effectiveness of their predictive models, *the retailer* implemented rigorous model evaluation and validation processes. They split their data into training and testing sets to assess model performance accurately. Metrics such as accuracy, precision, recall, and area under the curve (AUC) were used to evaluate model effectiveness. Additionally, they employed techniques such as cross-validation and grid search to fine-tune model parameters and optimize performance.

This dataset includes:

- *Customer ID:* A unique identifier for each customer.
- *Product ID:* A unique identifier for each product.
- *Category:* The category to which the product belongs.
- *Price (USD):* The price of the product.
- *Purchase Date:* The date when the purchase was made.

Sample Visualizations

Sales Volume by Product Category

This bar chart (*Figure 4.3*) shows the number of purchases for each category, illustrating the popularity of electronics, apparel, and home goods. Electronics appear to be the most frequently purchased category.

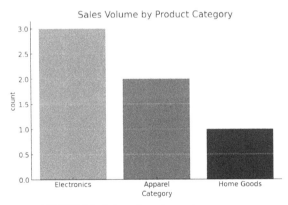

FIGURE 4.3. Sales volume by product category.

Total Revenue by Product Category

This bar chart (*Figure 4.3*) displays the total revenue generated from each product category. The electronics category significantly leads in revenue, reflecting both its higher price points and frequent purchases.

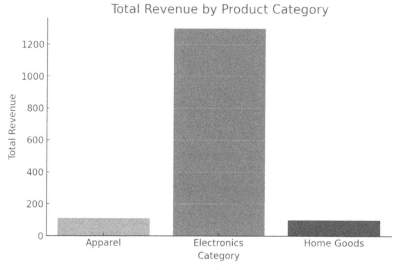

FIGURE 4.4. Total revenue by product category.

Price Distribution Within Each Category

The box plots (*Figure 4.5*) reveal the range and distribution of prices within each category. This visualization helps in understanding the pricing strategy for each category, with electronics showing a broader range of prices and higher values.

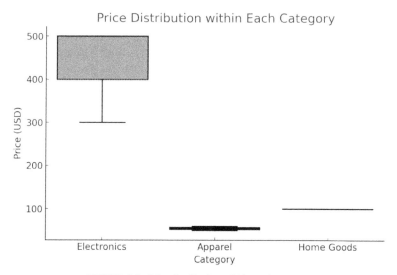

FIGURE 4.5. Price distribution within each category.

Python code

```
1   import pandas as pd
2   import seaborn as sns
3   import matplotlib.pyplot as plt
4
5   # Data setup
6   data_4 = {
7   "Customer ID": ["001", "002", "003", "004", "005", "006"], "Product ID": ["ABC123", "XYZ456", "LMN789", "ABC123", "PQR789",
8   }
9
10  df_4 = pd.DataFrame(data_4)
11
12  # Visualization: Sales Volume by Product Category
13  plt.figure(figsize=(8, 5))
14  sns.countplot(x='Category', data=df_4)
15  plt.title('Sales Volume by Product Category')
16  plt.show()
```

FIGURE 4.6. An example of Python code.

In this Python script, we use the "Pandas™," "Seaborn™," and "Matplotlib™" libraries to visualize sales volume data categorized by product category:

- *Data Setup*: The script structures data into a dictionary, including customer ID, product ID, product category, price, and purchase date. This is then converted into a Pandas DataFrame, providing a structured format suitable for data analysis and visualization.
- *Visualization*: The script creates a count plot that visualizes the number of purchases within each product category:
  - The "countplot" function from Seaborn is used, setting the product category as the x-axis. This function automatically counts the number of occurrences for each category, displaying them as bars.
  - The plot is set to 8x5 inches, ensuring the visualization is large enough to be easily readable.
  - The title "Sales Volume by Product Category" is used to clearly describe the focus of the plot.

This visualization is useful for quickly assessing which product categories are most popular based on the number of purchases, helping to identify consumer preferences or product demand trends.

By embracing predictive analytics and machine learning, the retailer revolutionized their approach to customer engagement. Through personalized recommendations powered by predictive models, they enhanced the shopping experience for customers, leading to increased satisfaction and loyalty. Moreover, by driving targeted promotions and cross-selling opportunities, the retailer achieved significant revenue growth and solidified their position as a leader in the competitive e-commerce landscape. This strategic use of technology not only improved customer retention but also attracted new customers, further expanding their market reach and reinforcing their reputation for innovation and customer-centricity in the digital marketplace.

IMPLEMENTATION ROADMAP: PREDICTIVE ANALYTICS AND MACHINE LEARNING

This implementation roadmap outlines a step-by-step process for applying in practice the predictive analytics and machine learning techniques presented in this chapter. This roadmap serves as a practical guide, providing clear instructions on how to collect, analyze, and interpret data to drive informed decision-making. It details the sequential steps necessary for executing projects, from the initial data acquisition to the deployment of predictive models. By following this guide, readers can methodically approach their data science projects, ensuring that each phase is managed with precision to optimize the outcomes of their analytical efforts. The roadmap is designed to help both novices and experienced practitioners streamline their workflows and achieve success in their predictive analytics endeavors.

Roadmap steps

- *Step 1*: Define predictive modeling objectives, select predictive modeling techniques, and prepare data for modeling.
- *Step 2*: Understand supervised learning and explore unsupervised learning.
- *Step 3*: Define evaluation metrics, perform model evaluation, and interpret results.

Step 1: Define Predictive Modeling Objectives, Select Predictive Modeling Techniques, and Prepare Data for Modeling

Step 1 sets the stage for predictive modeling endeavors by establishing clear objectives, whether it is forecasting sales, detecting anomalies, or predicting customer churn, selecting the most suitable techniques like regression or classification, and meticulously preparing the data through preprocessing steps like feature selection and data transformation to ensure model accuracy.

Define Predictive Modeling Objectives

Clearly define the objectives of predictive modeling, such as predicting customer churn, forecasting sales, or detecting anomalies. Establish specific, measurable goals to guide the development and evaluation of the models, ensuring they align with the strategic needs of the business.

Select Predictive Modeling Techniques

Identify appropriate predictive modeling techniques based on the nature of the problem, including regression, classification, time series analysis, or anomaly detection. Consider the characteristics of the data and the specific insights or predictions needed to address the business challenge effectively.

Prepare Data for Modeling

Preprocess and prepare the data for predictive modeling, including feature selection, data transformation, and splitting into training and testing sets. Ensure that the data is clean, relevant, and adequately formatted to maximize the performance and accuracy of the models developed.

Step 2: Understand Supervised Learning and Explore Unsupervised Learning

This section explores the realms of machine learning, beginning with supervised learning, where models learn from labeled data to predict outcomes like regression for continuous variables or classification for categories. Additionally, this section explores unsupervised learning techniques, where models uncover patterns or clusters from unlabeled data, including popular algorithms such as K-means and hierarchical clustering.

Understand Supervised Learning

Learn about supervised learning techniques, where the model learns from labeled data to make predictions, including regression for continuous outcomes and classification for categorical outcomes. This approach is fundamental for applications like fraud detection, customer segmentation, and health diagnosis, where historical data with known outcomes guides the learning process.

Explore Unsupervised Learning

Familiarize yourself with unsupervised learning techniques, where the model learns from unlabeled data to discover patterns or clusters, including clustering algorithms like K-means and hierarchical clustering. These techniques are essential for data exploration, market segmentation, and anomaly detection, where explicit labels are unavailable but patterns need to be identified.

Step 3: Define Evaluation Metrics, Perform Model Evaluation, and Interpret Results

Step 3 focuses on evaluating predictive models by choosing metrics like accuracy or precision, evaluating them using methods like cross-validation, and then interpreting the results to pick the best model for deployment.

Define Evaluation Metrics

Determine appropriate evaluation metrics based on the nature of the predictive modeling task, such as accuracy, precision, recall, F1-score, or mean squared error.

Perform Model Evaluation

Evaluate the performance of predictive models using cross-validation, holdout validation, or other validation techniques to assess their accuracy, robustness, and generalization ability. This step ensures that the model reliably predicts outcomes across various unseen data sets, helping to avoid overfitting and underperformance in practical applications.

Interpret Results

Interpret the results of model evaluation and validation to select the best-performing model and make informed decisions about deployment and implementation. Analyze metrics such as precision, recall, and ROC curves to understand the strengths and weaknesses of the model, ensuring that it aligns with business objectives and operational requirements.

By following this implementation roadmap, readers will be guided through the process of applying predictive analytics and machine learning techniques to solve real-world problems, from defining objectives and selecting appropriate techniques to evaluating and validating predictive models for deployment in practice. This comprehensive guide will help practitioners understand how to harness the power of data science to make better predictions, enhance decision-making, and optimize outcomes across various domains such as finance, healthcare, marketing, and more. It will ensure a structured approach to developing robust predictive models that are both effective and scalable.

CONCLUSION

By mastering the principles of predictive modeling, understanding supervised and unsupervised learning techniques, and following best practices for model evaluation and validation, organizations can harness the power of machine learning to extract valuable insights from data and make informed decisions. This chapter has provided the tools and knowledge needed to implement these techniques effectively, ensuring that practitioners can address a variety of business challenges and opportunities. As technology advances and data continues to grow in volume and complexity, the skills developed through this guide will remain crucial. Embracing these approaches will enable businesses to stay competitive, innovate, and adapt in an increasingly data-driven world, leading to smarter business strategies and improved operational efficiencies.

## CHAPTER 5

ETHICAL CONSIDERATIONS IN DATA SCIENCE

This chapter explores the ethical dimensions of data collection and usage, delving into issues of privacy, consent, data ownership, and responsible data practices. By respecting individuals' privacy rights, obtaining informed consent, clarifying data ownership and control, and prioritizing data security, organizations can navigate the ethical complexities of data collection and usage while minimizing potential risks and harm. It emphasizes the importance of transparent data practices, including clear communication with data subjects about how their information is used. These practices are crucial not only for legal compliance but also for maintaining public trust and the integrity of data-driven projects. By fostering a culture of ethics and responsibility, organizations can ensure they use data in ways that are both effective and ethical.

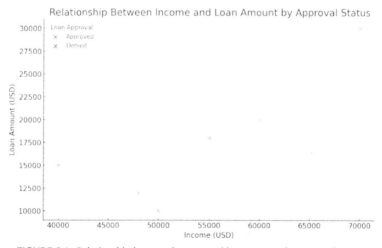

FIGURE 5.1. Relationship between income and loan amount by approval status.

Figure 5.1 is a scatter plot showing the relationship between income and loan amount, color-coded by loan approval status. Green dots represent approved loans, and red dots represent denied loans. This visualization can help in identifying any trends or patterns that might influence the loan approval process based on income and requested loan amounts.

Moving beyond data collection, this chapter explores the pervasive issues of fairness, bias, and transparency in algorithms and machine learning models. With the potential to perpetuate biases and inequities, algorithms must be designed and implemented with careful consideration for fairness and transparency. Through strategies such as fairness-aware techniques, bias detection and mitigation, transparency measures, and algorithmic impact assessments, organizations can mitigate the risks of bias and discrimination and promote accountability and trust in algorithmic decision-making processes.

Moreover, this section delves into the legal and regulatory frameworks that govern data science practices, encompassing data protection laws, anti-discrimination regulations, intellectual property rights, and regulatory compliance standards. By adhering to these frameworks and staying abreast of evolving legal requirements, organizations can ensure compliance with ethical standards and obligations, mitigate legal risks, and foster a culture of responsible and accountable data science practices. By addressing ethical considerations, promoting fairness and transparency, and adhering to legal and regulatory standards, organizations can uphold ethical standards, build trust among stakeholders, and harness the transformative potential of data science for the greater good.

ETHICS IN DATA COLLECTION AND USAGE

Data collection and usage raise important ethical questions regarding privacy, consent, and the potential for misuse of personal information. This section explores ethical considerations in data collection and usage.

Privacy and Consent

Respect individuals' right to privacy and obtain informed consent before collecting, storing, or processing their personal data. Provide clear and transparent information about the purpose of data collection, how the data will be used, and any potential risks or implications. It is essential to design privacy policies that are easily understandable and accessible, ensuring that consent is not only informed but also voluntary and explicit. This includes detailing any data sharing with third parties and the implications of such exchanges.

Data Ownership and Control

Clarify ownership and control rights over collected data, especially in cases where data is collected from multiple sources or shared with third parties. Ensure that individuals have the right to access, modify, or delete their personal data as needed. It is crucial to establish and communicate clear guidelines on data ownership, particularly when data is generated or enhanced through user interactions. Implement mechanisms that allow users to easily exercise their rights over their data, reinforcing their control and agency.

Data Security

Safeguard collected data against unauthorized access, disclosure, or misuse through robust security measures such as encryption, access controls, and regular security audits. Minimize the risk of data breaches and protect sensitive information from exploitation. Employ state-of-the-art security technologies and practices to ensure comprehensive protection of data integrity, confidentiality, and availability across all stages of data handling. Foster a culture of security within the organization to maintain ambitious standards of data protection.

Responsible Data Usage

Use the collected data responsibly and ethically, avoiding practices that may lead to harm, discrimination, or unfair treatment of individuals or groups. Consider the broader societal implications of data-driven decisions and strive to maximize societal benefit while minimizing potential harm. Implement frameworks for ethical decision-making that include stakeholder engagement and ethical reviews. Regularly evaluate the outcomes of data usage to ensure alignment with ethical standards and societal expectations, adjusting practices as necessary to prevent adverse impacts.

FAIRNESS, BIAS, AND TRANSPARENCY

Algorithms and machine learning models can inadvertently perpetuate biases and unfairness if not designed and implemented thoughtfully. This section examines strategies for promoting fairness, mitigating bias, and enhancing transparency in algorithms:

Fairness in Algorithm Design

Ensure that algorithms and models are designed to treat all individuals fairly and without bias, regardless of race, gender, ethnicity, or other protected characteristics. Consider fairness-aware techniques such as fairness constraints, fairness-aware regularization, and fairness-aware post-processing. Strive to integrate diverse perspectives and expert feedback during the algorithm design phase to better understand and address potential fairness issues. Regularly update and refine fairness criteria and algorithms based on new findings and societal changes, ensuring that fairness remains a dynamic component of algorithm design.

Bias Detection and Mitigation

Identify and mitigate biases in data, algorithms, and decision-making processes to prevent unfair outcomes. Use techniques such as bias auditing, bias mitigation algorithms, and debiasing strategies to address sources of bias and promote fairness. Regularly review and update data collection practices, model training procedures, and algorithm deployment strategies to ensure they do not inadvertently perpetuate or amplify biases. Involve diverse teams in the development and review of AI systems to gain broader perspectives on potential biases.

Transparency and Explainability

Enhance the transparency and explainability of algorithms to promote accountability, trust, and understanding among stakeholders. Provide clear explanations of how algorithms work, how decisions are made, and the potential implications for individuals affected by algorithmic decisions. Develop and share detailed documentation and user guides that explain the inner workings and decision-making processes of algorithms, ensuring that non-experts can also understand and assess the fairness and functionality of AI systems.

Algorithmic Impact Assessments

Conduct algorithmic impact assessments to evaluate the potential social, ethical, and legal implications of algorithmic systems. Assess the risks of bias, discrimination, and harm to ensure that algorithms are deployed responsibly and ethically. These assessments should be thorough, transparent, and regularly updated to reflect changes in the algorithm's design, application, or societal context. Engage with stakeholders, including those potentially impacted by the algorithm, to gain insights and address concerns proactively.

LEGAL AND REGULATORY FRAMEWORKS

Legal and regulatory frameworks play a crucial role in governing data science practices and ensuring compliance with ethical standards and obligations. This section examines key legal and regulatory considerations for data science:

Data Protection Laws

Comply with data protection laws and regulations, such as the General Data Protection Regulation (GDPR) in the European Union, the California Consumer Privacy Act (CCPA) in the United States, and similar regulations in other areas. Adhere to the principles of data minimization, purpose limitation, and data subject rights to protect individuals' privacy and data rights. Stay informed about changes in legislation and continuously adapt data handling practices to remain compliant. Educate all team members on the importance of data protection and the specific measures needed to secure data throughout its lifecycle.

Anti-Discrimination Laws

Avoid practices that may lead to discrimination or disparate impacts based on protected characteristics such as race, gender, age, or disability.

Ensure that algorithms and decision-making processes comply with anti-discrimination laws and regulations to prevent unfair treatment of individuals or groups. Regularly review and revise algorithms to eliminate any unintended biases and verify that decision-making processes are equitable across all demographics. Foster an organizational culture that prioritizes fairness and inclusivity in all data science practices.

Intellectual Property Rights

Respect intellectual property rights and data ownership rights when collecting, using, or sharing data. Obtain appropriate permissions and licenses for third-party data sources, and ensure that data usage complies with copyright, trademark, and other intellectual property laws. Establish clear guidelines for intellectual property management, including documenting the sources of data and the terms of use. Educate your team on the importance of adhering to intellectual property laws to protect the organization and the creators of original content.

Regulatory Compliance

Stay abreast of regulatory developments and updates relevant to data science practices, including industry-specific regulations and standards. Implement appropriate policies, procedures, and controls to ensure regulatory compliance and mitigate legal risks. Conduct regular audits to assess compliance with all applicable regulations and engage legal experts when necessary to navigate complex regulatory environments. Ensure that compliance efforts are scalable and adaptable to accommodate future regulatory changes and challenges.

USING ANALYTICS: ETHICAL CONSIDERATIONS IN DATA SCIENCE

This section focuses on using analytics and ethical considerations in data science, highlighting their efficacy in addressing complex challenges and driving informed decision-making, including:

Ethical Data Collection and Usage

Prioritize ethical considerations throughout the data lifecycle to ensure responsible data collection and usage practices. By adhering to ethical guidelines and obtaining informed consent from individuals, organizations can mitigate risks related to privacy violations and ensure the ethical handling of sensitive data. Organizations should develop comprehensive policies that outline acceptable data practices and train employees in ethical data handling. Establish protocols for responding to data breaches or unethical practices and conduct regular audits to ensure compliance with ethical standards. Such diligence fosters trust and maintains the integrity of data management processes.

Fairness, Bias, and Transparency

Address issues of fairness, bias, and transparency in analytics processes to promote equitable outcomes and build trust with stakeholders. By implementing fairness-aware algorithms, bias detection techniques, and transparency measures, organizations can identify and mitigate biases in data and algorithms, ensuring fairness and accountability in decision-making processes. Develop methodologies to routinely assess and adjust models to prevent discriminatory outcomes and ensure equitable treatment of all individuals. Foster an organizational culture that values transparency, allowing stakeholders to understand how decisions are made and promoting greater accountability.

Compliance with Legal and Regulatory Frameworks

Stay informed about the legal and regulatory frameworks governing data usage and privacy to ensure compliance and mitigate legal risks. By adhering to regulations such as GDPR, CCPA, and industry-specific standards, organizations can protect individuals' rights, minimize regulatory penalties, and maintain trust and credibility with customers and stakeholders. Implement a robust compliance management system that includes ongoing training for staff, regular policy updates, and technology solutions to monitor compliance. Engage with legal experts to navigate complex regulatory landscapes and adapt practices to meet evolving legal requirements effectively.

CASE STUDY: FAIR LENDING PRACTICES IN FINANCIAL SERVICES

In the financial services industry, ethical considerations play a critical role in ensuring fairness and transparency in lending practices. Let us explore how a leading bank navigated ethical challenges in data science to uphold fair lending principles and comply with regulatory requirements. This case study will detail the bank's initiative-taking measures for implementing robust data governance frameworks, enhancing algorithmic transparency, and instituting fairness audits. The bank's approach not only aligned with legal standards but also fostered trust and integrity in its operations, setting a benchmark for ethical practices in the highly scrutinized financial sector.

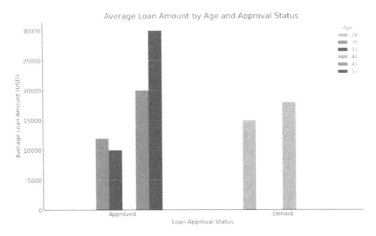

FIGURE 5.2. Average loan amount by age and approval status.

Figure 5.2 is a bar chart that shows the average loan amount by age for both approved and denied loan statuses. This visualization helps to identify how loan amounts vary by age and whether approval rates differ significantly across age groups.

Objective

A *leading bank* recognized the importance of ethical data collection and usage practices to prevent discrimination and uphold customer trust. They implemented strict protocols for data collection, ensuring transparency and consent from customers regarding the use of their personal information. Moreover, they established clear guidelines for the ethical handling and storage of sensitive customer data, prioritizing data security and privacy.

Approach

In the pursuit of fair lending practices, *a leading bank* prioritized the identification and mitigation of bias in their data-driven decision-making processes. They employed techniques such as fairness-aware machine learning algorithms and bias detection tools to identify and rectify potential biases in their lending models. Additionally, they maintained transparency by providing customers with clear explanations of the factors influencing lending decisions and offering avenues for recourse in case of disputes.

Result

Committed to compliance with legal and regulatory frameworks, *the bank* remained vigilant in navigating the complex landscape of financial regulations. They regularly monitored updates to laws such as the Equal Credit Opportunity Act (ECOA) and the Fair Credit Reporting Act (FCRA), ensuring their lending practices remained in accordance with legal requirements. Moreover, they collaborated with legal experts to interpret regulations accurately and implement necessary safeguards to protect customer rights.

TABLE 5.1. Bank bias mitigation data.

Customer ID	Age	Gender	Income (USD)	Loan Amount (USD)	Loan Approval
001	35	Male	50000	10000	Approved
002	45	Female	60000	20000	Approved
003	28	Male	40000	15000	Denied
004	55	Male	70000	30000	Approved
005	40	Female	55000	18000	Denied
006	30	Male	48000	12000	Approved

This dataset includes:

- *Customer ID*: A unique identifier for each customer.
- *Age*: Age of the customer.
- *Gender*: Gender of the customer.
- *Income (USD)*: Annual income of the customer.
- *Loan Amount (USD)*: The amount of the loan requested by the customer.
- *Loan Approval*: A binary indicator of whether the loan was approved or denied.

Sample Visualizations

Loan Approval Rates by Gender

This bar chart (*Figure 5.3*) displays the count of approved and denied loans split by gender. It provides a clear view of loan approval disparities between males and females, with males having a higher total number of loans approved.

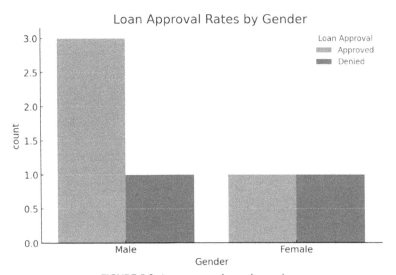

FIGURE 5.3. Loan approval rates by gender.

Income vs. Loan Amount with Approval Status

The scatter plot (*Figure 5.4*) shows the relationship between income and loan amounts, colored by approval status. This visualization helps identify if there is a pattern that suggests higher incomes correlate with higher loan amounts or better approval rates.

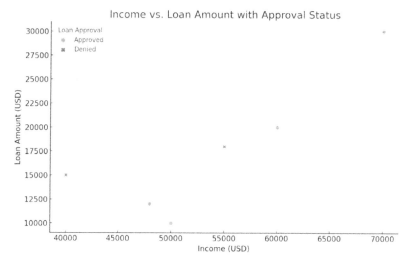

FIGURE 5.4. Income vs. loan amount with approval status.

Distribution of Loan Amounts by Approval Status

This histogram (*Figure 5.5*) stacks loan amounts by approval status, allowing you to see which loan amounts are more likely to be approved or denied. Loans around the middle of the amount range have mixed approval outcomes.

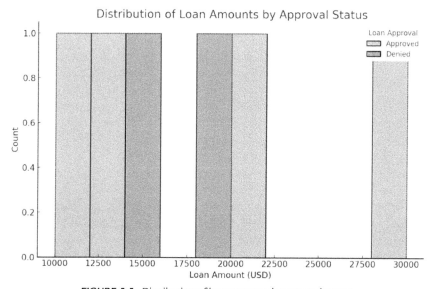

FIGURE 5.5. Distribution of loan amounts by approval status.

Python code

```
1   import pandas as pd
2   import seaborn as sns
3   import matplotlib.pyplot as plt
4
5   # Data setup
6   data_5 = {
7   "Customer ID": ["001", "002", "003", "004", "005", "006"], "Age": [35, 45, 28, 55, 40, 30], "Gender": ["Male", "Female",
8   }
9
10  df_5 = pd.DataFrame(data_5)
11
12  # Visualization: Loan Approval Rates by Gender
13  plt.figure(figsize=(8, 5))
14  sns.countplot(x='Gender', hue='Loan Approval', data=df_5)
15  plt.title('Loan Approval Rates by Gender')
16  plt.show()
```

FIGURE 5.6. An example of Python code.

This Python script utilizes the "Pandas™," "Seaborn™," and "Matplotlib™" libraries to create a visualization of loan approval rates categorized by gender:

- *Data Setup*: The script assembles data into a dictionary containing customer ID, age, gender, income, loan amount, and loan approval status. This dictionary is then converted into a Pandas DataFrame, which provides a structured and manipulatable format for analysis.
- *Visualization*: The script generates a count plot that displays the distribution of loan approvals for different genders:
  - The "countplot" function from Seaborn is employed, with gender as the x-axis and different loan approval statuses ("Approved" and "Denied") differentiated using the "hue" parameter. This creates a grouped bar chart.
  - The size of the plot is set to 8x5 inches to ensure the bars and labels are clear and legible.
  - The title "Loan Approval Rates by Gender" clearly indicates the focus of the plot, which is to show how loan approval varies between genders.

This visualization effectively highlights gender-based trends in loan approval within the dataset, providing insights into potential biases or patterns in financial decision-making.

By prioritizing ethical considerations in data science, a leading bank maintains trust and integrity in their lending practices. Through transparent data collection and usage practices, they upheld customer privacy and ensured fairness in lending decisions. By proactively addressing bias and complying with legal and regulatory frameworks, the bank not only mitigated reputational risks but also strengthened customer relationships and fostered a culture of ethical data-driven decision-making in the financial services industry. The bank's commitment to ethical standards was reflected in its rigorous data protection measures, adherence to fairness principles, and transparent communication with customers about how their data is used, significantly enhancing its reputation as a trustworthy institution.

IMPLEMENTATION ROADMAP: ETHICAL CONSIDERATIONS IN DATA SCIENCE

This implementation roadmap outlines a step-by-step process for applying in practice the data science and ethical considerations presented in this chapter. This roadmap serves as a practical guide, providing clear instructions on how to collect, analyze, and interpret data to drive informed decision-making. It emphasizes the importance of ethical data collection, ensuring transparency, fairness, and compliance with legal standards throughout the data lifecycle. Each step is designed to help practitioners not only achieve technical objectives but also uphold the highest ethical standards, thereby enhancing the credibility and impact of their data-driven initiatives. This comprehensive approach ensures that data science is conducted responsibly, fostering trust and integrity in data practices.

Roadmap steps

- *Step 1*: Establish ethical guidelines, conduct ethical impact assessments, and implement data governance frameworks.
- *Step 2*: Assess bias in data and algorithms, mitigate bias, and ensure transparency.
- *Step 3*: Stay informed about regulations, ensure compliance, and collaborate with legal experts.

Step 1: Establish Ethical Guidelines, Conduct Ethical Impact Assessments, and Implement Data Governance Frameworks

Step 1 lays the ethical groundwork for your data practices by setting clear guidelines, conducting assessments to anticipate ethical impacts, and implementing frameworks to govern data usage, ensuring adherence to principles like privacy and transparency.

Establish Ethical Guideline

Define ethical guidelines and principles for data collection and usage within your organization, emphasizing principles such as privacy, consent, and transparency. Establish a clear protocol for ensuring these guidelines are adhered to in every project, enhancing ethical compliance across all data-driven activities.

Conduct Ethical Impact Assessments

Perform ethical impact assessments to evaluate the potential ethical implications of data collection and usage practices, identify risks, and implement mitigating measures. These assessments should be integral to project planning and execution, ensuring that potential ethical issues are addressed proactively rather than reactively.

Implement Data Governance Frameworks

Develop and implement data governance frameworks to ensure compliance with ethical standards and regulations, including policies for data access, security, and privacy. Strengthen these frameworks with ongoing monitoring and evaluation mechanisms to adapt to new ethical challenges and regulatory changes as they arise.

Step 2: Assess Bias in Data and Algorithms, Mitigate Bias, and Ensure Transparency

Step 2 guides you through the crucial steps of identifying and addressing bias in both data and algorithms, employing techniques like data preprocessing and algorithm adjustments, while also emphasizing transparency by documenting methodologies and disclosing data sources.

Assess Bias in Data and Algorithms

Evaluate the presence of bias in data and algorithms used for decision-making, including demographic bias, algorithmic bias, and unintended consequences. Regularly review and audit data sets and algorithms to identify and understand the sources of bias that may affect outcomes and assess the impact these biases have on distinct groups.

Mitigate Bias

Implement strategies to mitigate bias in data and algorithms, such as data preprocessing techniques, algorithmic adjustments, and fairness-aware machine learning models. Develop and deploy de-biasing techniques across all stages of the data science lifecycle to ensure fairer outcomes and reduce the risk of discrimination in automated decisions.

Ensure Transparency

Promote transparency in data science processes and decision-making by documenting methodologies, disclosing data sources and limitations, and providing explanations for model predictions. Establish protocols to ensure that stakeholders can understand and challenge the decisions made by AI systems, thereby building trust and accountability in data-driven applications.

Step 3: Stay Informed about Regulations, Ensure Compliance, and Collaborate with Legal Experts

Step 3 emphasizes the importance of staying updated on regulations such as GDPR and CCPA, ensuring compliance through measures like data anonymization, and collaborating with legal experts to interpret regulations accurately and manage risks effectively.

Stay Informed about Regulations

Keep abreast of legal and regulatory frameworks governing data collection, usage, and privacy, including regulations such as GDPR, CCPA, HIPAA, and industry-specific standards. Regular updates and training sessions can help maintain awareness and readiness to adapt to new regulatory changes and global privacy standards.

Ensure Compliance

Ensure compliance with legal and regulatory requirements by implementing measures such as data anonymization, consent management, data breach reporting, and user rights enforcement. Regular audits and compliance checks can help identify potential areas of non-compliance and allow for timely corrective actions to safeguard data and maintain regulatory adherence.

Collaborate with Legal Experts

Collaborate with legal experts to interpret regulations accurately, assess legal risks, and develop strategies for compliance and risk management. This collaboration should also focus on the ongoing review and adaptation of practices to meet evolving legal standards, ensuring that data usage aligns with both current laws and emerging legal trends.

By following this implementation roadmap, organizations can effectively address ethical considerations in data science, ensuring responsible and ethical practices in data collection, usage, and decision-making while also complying with legal and regulatory requirements. This comprehensive approach helps establish a culture of integrity and transparency, strengthens stakeholder trust, and enhances the overall credibility and effectiveness of data-driven initiatives. Organizations will not only protect themselves from legal and reputational risks but also set a standard for ethical conduct that can serve as a competitive advantage in the industry.

CONCLUSION

By addressing ethical considerations in data collection and usage, promoting fairness, bias mitigation, and transparency in algorithms, and adhering to legal and regulatory frameworks, organizations can uphold ethical standards, foster trust among stakeholders, and ensure responsible and accountable use of data science technologies. This diligent approach minimizes the risks of misuse and discrimination, enhances the reliability of analytical outcomes, and promotes a culture of ethical awareness and compliance. Furthermore, by prioritizing these values, organizations not only safeguard their operational integrity but also contribute positively to the broader societal impacts of technology. Such responsible practices are crucial for maintaining public confidence and driving sustainable innovation in an increasingly data-driven world.

CHAPTER 6

BUILDING A DATA-DRIVEN CULTURE

In today's data-centric landscape, cultivating a culture that embraces data-driven decision-making is imperative for organizations seeking to thrive in a rapidly evolving environment. This chapter serves as a roadmap for organizations looking to build a robust data-driven culture, focusing on strategies for fostering data literacy, overcoming organizational challenges, and implementing data-driven decision-making processes. It emphasizes the importance of leadership commitment to data-centric values and the need for ongoing education to enhance employees' analytical skills. Additionally, it discusses the integration of advanced data analytics into everyday business practices to improve decision-making accuracy and operational efficiency. By embracing these strategies, organizations can harness the full potential of their data assets and drive meaningful business outcomes.

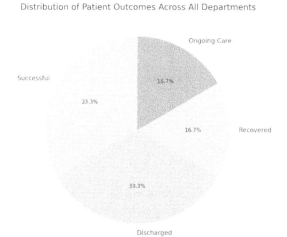

FIGURE 6.1. Distribution of patient outcomes across all departments.

Figure 6.1 is a pie chart showing the distribution of patient outcomes across all departments. This visualization helps us to understand the proportion of various outcomes such as successful treatments, recoveries, discharges, and ongoing care within the hospital.

At the heart of a data-driven culture lies data literacy—the ability of individuals across the organization to understand, interpret, and communicate data effectively. This chapter explores various strategies for fostering data literacy, including providing education and training opportunities, promoting continuous learning, offering firsthand experience, and garnering leadership support. By empowering employees with the skills and knowledge to navigate data effectively, organizations can lay the foundation for data-driven decision-making at all levels.

However, implementing a data-driven culture is not without its challenges. Organizational barriers such as resistance to change, siloed data, and resource constraints can impede progress. This chapter considers strategies for overcoming these challenges, emphasizing the importance of change management, data integration and governance, resource allocation, and defining clear metrics and KPIs. By addressing these challenges head-on and fostering a collaborative and inclusive environment, organizations can create the conditions necessary for a thriving data-driven culture.

Moreover, this chapter explores the practical aspects of implementing data-driven decision-making processes, from defining clear objectives to collecting and analyzing data, developing decision support systems, and fostering a culture of iterative improvement and learning. By integrating data analytics seamlessly into existing workflows and decision-making frameworks, organizations can unlock the full potential of their data assets and drive innovation, optimize performance, and achieve strategic objectives.

Ultimately, building a data-driven culture is an ongoing journey that requires commitment, collaboration, and continuous improvement at all levels of the organization. By embracing data literacy, overcoming organizational challenges, and implementing data-driven decision-making processes, organizations can harness the power of data to navigate complexity, seize opportunities, and chart a course for sustainable growth and success in the digital age.

FOSTERING A CULTURE OF DATA LITERACY

Data literacy is the ability to understand, interpret, and communicate data effectively. This section discusses strategies for fostering a culture of data literacy within organizations:

Education and Training

Provide employees with training and educational resources to enhance their data literacy skills. Offer workshops, courses, and certification programs covering topics such as data analysis, statistics, visualization, and data ethics. These programs should be tailored to meet the diverse needs of employees across different departments, ensuring that everyone, from marketing to operations, gains a fundamental understanding of how data can drive decision-making.

Promote Continuous Learning

Encourage a culture of continuous learning and skill development by providing opportunities for employees to expand their knowledge and expertise in data-related fields. Support participation in online courses, conferences, and professional development activities. Foster an environment where learning is recognized and rewarded and where employees are motivated to stay current with emerging data technologies and analytical techniques.

Firsthand Experience

Provide employees with firsthand experience working with data through real-world projects, case studies, and collaborative initiatives. Encourage cross-functional collaboration and knowledge sharing to facilitate learning and skill development. This practical experience helps employees understand the impact of data insights on business outcomes and promotes a first-hand approach to solving complex business challenges.

Leadership Support

Cultivate leadership support and sponsorship for data literacy initiatives to demonstrate the importance of data-driven decision-making and encourage organizational buy-in. Empower leaders to lead by example and champion data-driven practices within their teams. Ensure that leaders are actively involved in setting strategic goals that align with data initiatives, providing necessary resources, and removing obstacles to data literacy advancement.

OVERCOMING ORGANIZATIONAL CHALLENGES

Implementing a data-driven culture may encounter various organizational challenges, including resistance to change, siloed data, and limited resources. This section explores strategies for overcoming these challenges:

Change Management

Address resistance to change by fostering a culture of openness, collaboration, and inclusivity. Communicate the benefits of data-driven decision-making clearly and regularly to all employees. Involve them in the decision-making process by soliciting feedback and incorporating their insights, which helps build consensus and alignment. Implement structured change management programs to support employees through the transition, providing training and resources to ease the adoption of new data-driven practices.

Data Integration and Governance

Break down data silos and promote robust data integration and governance practices to ensure data accessibility, consistency, and reliability across the organization. Implement standardized data governance frameworks that outline clear data ownership, stewardship, and accountability mechanisms. Regularly audit data processes to maintain data quality and integrity, and establish cross-functional data governance committees to oversee and manage data-related initiatives.

Resource Allocation

Allocate sufficient resources, including funding, technology, and talent, to support data-driven initiatives and infrastructure development. Ensure that budgetary allocations prioritize investments in data analytics capabilities, tools, and platforms that align with strategic objectives and deliver measurable value. Develop a talent acquisition and development strategy to attract and retain skilled data professionals and provide ongoing training to enhance the capabilities of existing staff.

Metrics and KPIs

Define key performance indicators (KPIs) and metrics to track the progress and impact of data-driven initiatives. Establish clear goals, benchmarks, and success criteria to measure the effectiveness of data-driven decision-making and drive accountability. Use these metrics to create dashboards and reports that provide real-time insights into performance, enabling timely adjustments and continuous improvement. Communicate these metrics regularly to all stakeholders to ensure transparency and foster a purposeful culture.

IMPLEMENTING DATA-DRIVEN DECISION MAKING

Implementing data-driven decision-making processes involves integrating data analytics into existing workflows and decision-making frameworks. This chapter discusses strategies for implementing data-driven decision-making.

Define Clear Objectives

Clearly define the objectives and goals of data-driven decision-making initiatives, aligning them with the organization's strategic priorities and business objectives. Ensure that these objectives are specific, measurable, achievable, relevant, and time-bound (SMART) to provide clear direction and facilitate effective tracking of progress and outcomes.

Data Collection and Analysis

Collect relevant data from internal and external sources, ensuring comprehensive coverage of all necessary information. Clean, preprocess, and analyze the data to extract actionable insights. Utilize advanced data analytics techniques and tools, such as machine learning algorithms and statistical analysis, to uncover patterns, trends, and relationships within the data, driving informed decision-making.

Decision Support Systems

Develop robust decision support systems and tools that seamlessly integrate data analytics capabilities into existing workflows and decision-making processes. Provide decision-makers with access to intuitive dashboards, detailed reports, and interactive visualizations that facilitate real-time data-driven decision-making. Ensure that these systems are user-friendly and customizable to meet the diverse needs of different stakeholders.

Iterative Improvement

Continuously monitor and evaluate the effectiveness of data-driven decision-making processes, soliciting feedback from stakeholders at all levels. Use this feedback to identify areas for improvement and implement necessary changes. Incorporate lessons learned from past experiences to refine methodologies, enhance data quality, and drive continuous improvement in decision-making practices.

Cultivate a Learning Culture

Foster a culture of experimentation, innovation, and learning by encouraging data-driven experimentation and calculated risk-taking. Embrace failure as an opportunity for learning and improvement, providing support and resources to help employees learn from their experiences. Celebrate successes and share case studies to reinforce the value of data-driven decision-making, promoting a culture that values continuous learning and adaptation.

USING ANALYTICS: BUILDING A DATA-DRIVEN CULTURE

This section focuses on using analytics and building a data-driven culture, highlighting their efficacy in addressing complex challenges and driving informed decision-making, including:

Fostering a Culture of Data Literacy

Promote data literacy among employees to empower them to effectively leverage analytics in their roles. By providing training, resources, and support for data literacy initiatives, organizations can cultivate a workforce that is knowledgeable about data concepts, tools, and techniques, fostering a culture of data-driven decision-making and innovation. Encourage cross-departmental learning, set up data literacy champions, and create a centralized knowledge repository to support continuous learning and skill development across the organization.

Overcoming Organizational Challenges

Address organizational challenges that may hinder the adoption of data-driven approaches. By identifying and mitigating barriers such as resistance to change, siloed data, and a lack of executive buy-in, organizations can create an environment conducive to data-driven innovation and collaboration, enabling the successful implementation of analytics initiatives. Conduct organizational assessments to pinpoint specific challenges, establish change management programs, and engage leadership in championing data initiatives to drive cultural and structural change.

Implementing Data-Driven Decision Making

Embed data-driven decision-making processes into organizational workflows to drive strategic outcomes and performance improvements. By integrating analytics tools and techniques into decision-making frameworks, organizations can leverage data insights to inform strategic planning, optimize operations, and drive innovation, enhancing business performance and competitiveness. Develop comprehensive data governance policies, invest in advanced analytics platforms, and establish clear protocols for data access and usage to ensure consistent, informed decision-making across all levels of the organization.

CASE STUDY: CULTIVATING DATA LITERACY IN A HEALTHCARE ORGANIZATION

In the healthcare sector, fostering a data-driven culture is essential for improving patient outcomes and operational efficiency. Let us explore how *a leading hospital network* embraced data literacy and implemented data-driven decision-making processes to enhance healthcare delivery. By investing in advanced analytics tools, providing extensive training to healthcare professionals, and promoting a culture of continuous learning, the hospital network was able to harness the power of data. This enabled them to identify trends, optimize resource allocation, and personalize patient care, leading to improved clinical outcomes and increased patient satisfaction. The case study highlights the transformative impact of data-driven strategies on healthcare systems.

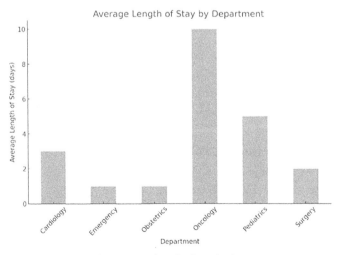

FIGURE 6.2. Average length of stay by department.

Figure 6.2 is a bar chart that shows the average length of stay by department. This visualization helps to identify which departments have longer or shorter average stays, which can be indicative of several types of patient care dynamics.

Objective

A *leading hospital network* recognized the importance of promoting data literacy among staff to enable informed decision-making at all levels of the organization. They implemented comprehensive training programs and workshops to enhance staff's understanding of data concepts and analytics tools. By providing access to educational resources and firsthand training sessions, they empowered employees to leverage data effectively in their day-to-day roles.

Approach

Transitioning to a data-driven culture posed several challenges for *a leading hospital network*, including resistance to change and siloed data systems. To address these challenges, they emphasized the importance of cross-functional collaboration and communication. They established interdisciplinary teams to break down silos and foster collaboration between departments. Additionally, they implemented data governance frameworks to ensure data quality, consistency, and security across the organization.

Result

The hospital network integrated data-driven decision-making processes into their organizational workflows to drive continuous improvement in healthcare delivery. They leveraged data analytics tools and dashboards to monitor key performance indicators (KPIs) related to patient outcomes, resource utilization, and operational efficiency. By analyzing data in real-time, they identified areas for improvement and implemented evidence-based interventions to enhance patient care and streamline operations.

TABLE 6.1. Hospital network data literacy data.

Date	Department	Patient ID	Diagnosis	Treatment	Length of Stay	Outcome
1/1/2024	Cardiology	001	Coronary Artery Disease	Angioplasty	3	Successful
1/1/2024	Pediatrics	002	Pneumonia	Antibiotics	5	Recovered
1/1/2024	Emergency	003	Fractured Arm	Casting	1	Discharged
1/2/2024	Surgery	004	Appendicitis	Appendectomy	2	Successful
1/2/2024	Obstetrics	005	Normal Delivery	NA	1	Discharged
1/2/2024	Oncology	006	Breast Cancer	Chemotherapy	10	Ongoing Care

This dataset includes:

- *Date*: The date of patient admission or treatment.
- *Department*: The department within the hospital where the patient was treated.
- *Patient ID*: A unique identifier for each patient.
- *Diagnosis*: The medical condition or diagnosis of the patient.
- *Treatment*: The treatment administered to the patient.
- *Length of Stay (Days)*: The number of days the patient stayed in the hospital.
- *Outcome*: The outcome of the treatment (e.g., successful, recovered, discharged, ongoing care).

Sample Visualizations

Length of Stay by Department

The box plot (*Figure 6.3*) provides a visual comparison of the length of stay distributions across different departments. It reveals variations in stay duration, which can be associated with the nature of medical issues treated by each department.

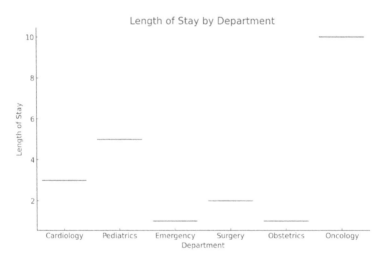

FIGURE 6.3. Length of stay by department.

Outcomes by Diagnosis

This stacked bar chart (*Figure 6.4*) displays the outcomes associated with each diagnosis, illustrating how different medical conditions result in varied outcomes like "Successful," "Recovered," "Discharged," or "Ongoing Care." It helps to see the effectiveness of treatments across different diagnoses.

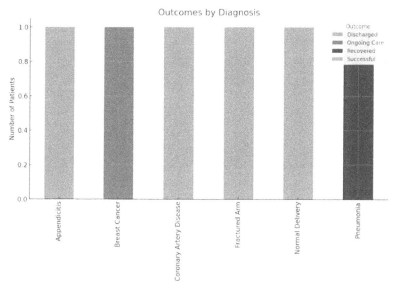

FIGURE 6.4. Outcomes by diagnosis.

Number of Treatments by Department

The bar chart (*Figure 6.5*) shows the number of treatments administered by each department. It highlights the volume of cases managed by each department, with some handling more than others, reflecting departmental workloads or patient inflow.

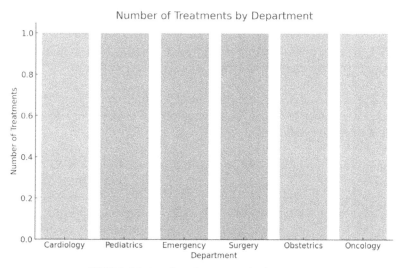

FIGURE 6.5. Number of treatments by department.

Python code

```
1   import pandas as pd
2   import seaborn as sns
3   import matplotlib.pyplot as plt
4
5   # Data setup
6   data_6 = {
7   "Date": ["1/1/2024", "1/1/2024", "1/1/2024", "1/2/2024", "1/2/2024", "1/2/2024"], "Department": ["Cardiology", "Pediatrics"
8   }
9
10  df_6 = pd.DataFrame(data_6)
11
12  # Visualization: Length of Stay by Department
13  plt.figure(figsize=(10, 6))
14  sns.boxplot(x='Department', y='Length of Stay', data=df_6)
15  plt.title('Length of Stay by Department')
16  plt.show()
```

FIGURE 6.6. An example of Python code.

This Python script uses the "Pandas™," "Seaborn™," and "Matplotlib™" libraries to visualize the length of patient stays across different hospital departments:

- *Data Setup*: The script organizes data into a dictionary that includes the date, department, patient ID, diagnosis, treatment, length of stay, and outcome. This dictionary is then converted into a pandas DataFrame for structured data manipulation.
- *Visualization*: The script creates a boxplot to represent the distribution of patient stay lengths for each department:
  - The "boxplot" function from Seaborn is used, setting "Department" as the x-axis and "Length of Stay" as the y-axis. This plot type is particularly effective for displaying the range, median, quartiles, and potential outliers in the data.
  - The plot dimensions are set to 10x6 inches to ensure all department labels and the boxplot details are clearly visible.
  - The title "Length of Stay by Department" succinctly conveys the focus of the visualization, allowing viewers to easily interpret differences and variations in patient stay durations across departments.

This visualization is useful for hospital administrators to identify trends, assess departmental efficiencies, and pinpoint areas needing process improvement or resource allocation.

IMPLEMENTATION ROADMAP: BUILDING A DATA-DRIVEN CULTURE

This implementation roadmap outlines a step-by-step process for applying the techniques presented in this chapter to build a data-driven culture. This roadmap serves as a practical guide, providing clear instructions on how to collect, analyze, and interpret data to drive informed decision-making. By following these steps, organizations can ensure they are effectively leveraging data to enhance strategic planning, optimize operations, and foster a culture of continuous improvement. This approach not only empowers employees to utilize data in their daily roles but also aligns data-driven initiatives with broader organizational goals, promoting sustained growth and innovation.

Roadmap Steps

- *Step 1*: Assess current data literacy levels, provide training and development, and promote continuous learning.
- *Step 2*: Identify organizational barriers, foster cross-functional collaboration, and foster cross-functional collaboration.
- *Step 3*: Define data-driven objectives, develop data governance frameworks, and integrate data into decision-making processes.

Step 1: Assess Current Data Literacy Levels, Provide Training and Development, and Promote Continuous Learning

Step 1 begins by gauging the current understanding of data within the organization through surveys or interviews to pinpoint areas for growth. Following this assessment, tailored training sessions and resources to boost data literacy are offered, fostering a culture of ongoing learning and knowledge sharing to keep pace with evolving trends and technologies.

Assess Current Data Literacy Levels

Evaluate the existing data literacy levels within the organization through surveys, assessments, or interviews to identify areas for improvement. This evaluation should encompass all departments to gain a comprehensive understanding of the organization's strengths and weaknesses in data literacy.

Provide Training and Development

Offer training programs, workshops, and resources to enhance data literacy skills among employees, covering topics such as data interpretation, visualization, and analysis. These programs should be tailored to different skill levels and roles to ensure that all employees benefit from the training.

Promote Continuous Learning

Encourage a culture of continuous learning and knowledge sharing around data literacy, providing opportunities for employees to expand their skills and stay updated on emerging trends and technologies. Establish regular training sessions, Webinars, and access to online courses to maintain engagement and knowledge growth.

Step 2: Identify Organizational Barriers, Foster Cross-Functional Collaboration, and Address Change Management

Step 2 tackles organizational hurdles by pinpointing barriers such as resistance to change or data silos and promoting cross-departmental collaboration to foster shared understanding and cooperation in data initiatives.

Identify Organizational Barriers

Identify organizational barriers that may hinder the adoption of data-driven approaches, such as resistance to change, lack of resources, or siloed data. Conduct thorough assessments and gather feedback from various departments to pinpoint these obstacles and understand their root causes.

Foster Cross-Functional Collaboration

Promote cross-functional collaboration and communication to break down silos and facilitate knowledge sharing and collaboration around data initiatives. Encourage teams from different departments to work together on data projects, leveraging diverse expertise to drive innovation and improve decision-making.

Address Change Management

Implement change management strategies to overcome resistance to change and foster buy-in from stakeholders, including clear communication, leadership support, and employee engagement initiatives. Develop comprehensive plans that address concerns, provide training, and highlight the benefits of transitioning to a data-driven culture, ensuring a smooth and successful adoption process.

Step 3: Define Data-Driven Objectives, Develop Data Governance Frameworks, and Integrate Data into Decision-Making Processes

Step 3 is about leveraging data effectively by setting clear goals, ensuring data quality and security, and seamlessly integrating data insights into decision-making processes across the organization.

Define Data-Driven Objectives

Clearly define objectives and key performance indicators (KPIs) that will guide data-driven decision-making efforts, aligning them with organizational goals and priorities. Ensure these objectives are specific, measurable, achievable, relevant, and time-bound (SMART) to provide a clear roadmap for success and enable effective tracking of progress.

Develop Data Governance Frameworks

Establish data governance frameworks to ensure data quality, integrity, and security, including policies and procedures for data collection, storage, and usage. Implement roles and responsibilities for data stewardship, create data standards, and develop protocols for data access and sharing to maintain consistency and trustworthiness.

Integrate Data into Decision-Making Processes

Embed data-driven decision-making processes into organizational workflows and decision-making frameworks, providing access to data insights and analytics tools to enable informed decision-making at all levels. Foster a culture where data is a key component of strategic planning and operational decisions, supported by regular training and resources to enhance data literacy and analytical skills across the organization.

By following this implementation roadmap, organizations can foster a culture of data literacy, overcome organizational challenges, and implement data-driven decision-making processes effectively, driving innovation, performance, and competitiveness through data-driven approaches. This roadmap provides clear guidelines and actionable steps, ensuring that all employees are equipped with the necessary skills and knowledge to leverage data effectively. By promoting continuous learning, fostering cross-functional collaboration, and integrating data into everyday decision-making processes, organizations can unlock the full potential of their data assets, leading to more informed strategic planning, optimized operations, and sustained competitive advantage in an increasingly data-centric world.

CONCLUSION

By fostering a culture of data literacy, overcoming organizational challenges, and implementing data-driven decision-making processes, organizations can harness the power of data to drive innovation, optimize performance, and achieve strategic objectives. Building a data-driven culture is an ongoing journey that requires commitment, collaboration, and continuous improvement at all levels of the organization. This journey begins with a clear understanding of the current data literacy levels, followed by targeted training and development programs to enhance employees' data skills. It also involves addressing organizational barriers, promoting cross-functional collaboration, and implementing robust data governance frameworks to ensure data quality and security. By embedding data-driven decision-making into everyday workflows, organizations can make informed decisions that drive strategic planning and operational efficiency. Continuous learning and adaptation are essential as the data landscape evolves rapidly. Organizations must stay updated on emerging trends and technologies to maintain a competitive edge. A data-driven culture empowers organizations to transform data into valuable insights, fostering an initiative-taking and innovative environment that supports long-term growth and success.

## CHAPTER 7

CASE STUDIES IN DATA-DRIVEN SUCCESS

C ase studies serve as powerful illustrations of how organizations have harnessed data-driven approaches to achieve remarkable success across various industries. This chapter delves into industry-specific case studies, drawing out invaluable lessons learned, best practices, and practical insights for decision-makers eager to implement data-driven strategies. By examining real-world examples, readers can gain a deeper understanding of how to effectively apply data analytics to solve complex business challenges. These case studies highlight the transformative impact of data-driven decision-making, highlighting the tangible benefits and competitive advantages that can be achieved. Additionally, they provide actionable takeaways that can be adapted to various organizational contexts, ensuring a comprehensive understanding of the practical implementation of data-driven approaches.

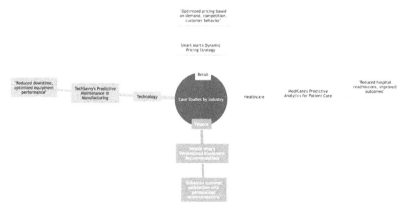

FIGURE 7.1. Mindmap: Industries and strategies outlined in case studies.

Figure 7.1 is a mindmap to illustrate the connections between industries and their strategies outlined in the case studies. This will provide a clear and structured visualization of how each industry is leveraging technology.

Across retail, healthcare, finance, manufacturing, and marketing, organizations have demonstrated the transformative impact of data-driven approaches. For instance, the recommendation engine of Amazon™ has revolutionized personalized shopping experiences, while IBM Watson Health™ has leveraged advanced analytics to drive personalized healthcare interventions. Similarly, the use of data analytics by PayPal™ has bolstered fraud detection in finance, and the predictive maintenance algorithms of General Electric™ have optimized operations in manufacturing. Furthermore, Netflix™ has leveraged data analytics to inform content recommendations and personalized marketing campaigns in the entertainment industry.

From these case studies emerge crucial lessons and best practices. Organizations that prioritize data quality and governance, foster cross-functional collaboration, embrace agile and iterative approaches, and uphold ethical considerations tend to excel in their data-driven initiatives. Decision-makers play a pivotal role in driving these initiatives forward. Leadership support, talent acquisition and development, measurement of impact and ROI, and a culture of continuous improvement are key factors that contribute to the success of data-driven strategies.

Through examining these case studies, distilling their insights, and applying practical recommendations, organizations can embark on their own data-driven journey with confidence. Building a data-driven culture is a journey marked by commitment, collaboration, and continuous improvement, but the dividends of data-driven success are profound and enduring.

INDUSTRY-SPECIFIC CASE STUDIES

Data-driven success stories span across various industries, from retail and healthcare to finance and manufacturing. This section explores industry-specific case studies highlighting the transformative power of data-driven approaches:

Retail

The recommendation engine of Amazon is a prime example of data-driven personalization, leveraging customer data to deliver personalized product recommendations and enhance the shopping experience. This sophisticated system analyzes users' past purchases, browsing history, and even items they have added to their wish list. By doing so, it predicts products that customers are likely to be interested in, thereby increasing the likelihood of purchase. This personalized approach not only improves the customer experience by making shopping more convenient but also significantly boosts the sales and customer retention rates of Amazon. The recommendation engine's success is attributed to its use of advanced algorithms and machine learning techniques that continually refine and improve the accuracy of recommendations based on ongoing user interactions and feedback.

Healthcare

IBM Watson Health utilizes advanced analytics and artificial intelligence to analyze medical data and provide insights for personalized healthcare interventions, diagnosis, and treatment planning. Watson Health aggregates and examines vast amounts of clinical data, medical literature, and patient records to assist healthcare professionals in making more informed decisions. For instance, in oncology, Watson Health can suggest potential treatment options by cross-referencing patient data with existing medical research and clinical trial outcomes. This technology aids in identifying the most effective treatment protocols tailored to individual patients, thereby improving outcomes and reducing the trial-and-error approach traditionally associated with medical treatment. Additionally, by continuously learning from new data, IBM Watson Health helps healthcare providers stay abreast of the latest medical advancements and treatment methodologies.

Finance

PayPal uses data analytics and machine learning algorithms to detect and prevent fraudulent transactions, minimizing risks and protecting users' financial assets. The company's fraud detection system analyzes a vast array of data points, including transaction history, user behavior patterns, and real-time payment activity, to identify suspicious activities. By employing machine learning models, PayPal can detect anomalies that may indicate fraudulent behavior, such as unusual transaction amounts or atypical account access locations. This initiative-taking approach allows PayPal to block potentially fraudulent transactions before they are completed, thereby safeguarding users' accounts and maintaining trust in their financial services. The continuous refinement of these models ensures they adapt to evolving fraud tactics while maintaining robust security measures.

Manufacturing

General Electric (GE) employs predictive maintenance algorithms to analyze sensor data from industrial equipment and optimize maintenance schedules, reducing downtime and increasing operational efficiency. These predictive maintenance systems use data collected from sensors embedded in machinery to monitor performance indicators such as temperature, vibration, and pressure. By analyzing this data, GE can predict when equipment is likely to fail and schedule maintenance before breakdowns occur. This initiative-taking maintenance approach helps to avoid unplanned outages, extends the lifespan of machinery, and reduces maintenance costs. Additionally, it enables GE to optimize inventory management for spare parts and improve overall production planning, enhancing operational efficiency and productivity across their manufacturing operations.

Marketing

Netflix leverages data analytics and machine learning algorithms to analyze user behavior and preferences, informing content recommendations, personalized marketing campaigns, and original content production. By examining viewing history, search queries, and user ratings, Netflix can create highly personalized viewing experiences for each subscriber. This data-driven approach helps Netflix suggest movies and TV shows that align with individual preferences, thereby increasing user engagement and satisfaction. Furthermore, insights gained from data analysis guide Netflix in deciding which original content to produce, ensuring that new shows and movies meet audience demand. Personalized marketing campaigns tailored to user preferences also help Netflix attract and retain subscribers, solidifying its position as a leader in the streaming industry.

LESSONS LEARNED AND BEST PRACTICES

Successful data-driven initiatives share common themes and best practices that contribute to their effectiveness. This section distills lessons learned and highlights best practices from the case studies:

Data Quality and Governance

Invest in data quality and governance processes to ensure that data is accurate, dependable, and trustworthy. Establishing clear data governance policies, standards, and procedures is crucial for maintaining data integrity and consistency across the organization. This includes implementing rigorous data validation checks, regular audits, and data cleaning processes to remove inaccuracies and inconsistencies. By doing so, organizations can ensure that decision-makers have access to reliable data, which is essential for making informed decisions. Additionally, setting up a data governance framework that defines roles and responsibilities, data stewardship, and compliance with regulatory requirements helps in managing data effectively and protecting sensitive information.

Cross-Functional Collaboration

Foster collaboration and communication across functional teams and departments to break down silos and leverage diverse perspectives and expertise. Encourage cross-functional teams to work together on data-driven projects, bringing together unique insights and skills from different areas of the organization. This collaborative approach not only drives innovation but also ensures that data initiatives are aligned with the overall strategic goals of the company. Regular cross-departmental meetings, collaborative tools, and team-building activities can enhance communication and foster a culture of teamwork. By leveraging the collective knowledge and experience of various teams, organizations can achieve more comprehensive and effective, data-driven solutions.

Agile and Iterative Approach

Embrace an agile and iterative approach to data-driven decision-making, allowing for experimentation, rapid prototyping, and continuous improvement. This methodology enables organizations to quickly evaluate hypotheses, gather feedback, and refine their data strategies based on real-world outcomes. By iterating on data-driven solutions, businesses can adapt to changing market conditions and business needs more effectively. An agile approach encourages flexibility, responsiveness, and a focus on incremental progress, which is vital for fostering innovation. Regularly reviewing and adjusting strategies based on performance metrics and user feedback helps ensure that data-driven initiatives remain relevant and impactful.

Ethical Considerations

Prioritize ethical considerations and responsible data practices throughout the data lifecycle, from collection and analysis to decision-making and deployment. Uphold principles of fairness, transparency, and accountability to mitigate risks and ensure ethical use of data. This includes obtaining informed consent from data subjects, ensuring data privacy, and implementing measures to prevent bias in data analysis and algorithm development. Ethical data practices build trust with stakeholders and protect the organization from legal and reputational risks. Establishing an ethics committee, conducting regular ethical audits, and developing clear guidelines for ethical data usage can help organizations navigate the complexities of data ethics and maintain public trust.

PRACTICAL INSIGHTS FOR DECISION MAKERS

Decision-makers play a crucial role in driving data-driven initiatives and fostering a culture of data-driven decision-making within their organizations. This section provides practical insights and recommendations for decision-makers:

Leadership Support

Demonstrate leadership support and commitment to data-driven initiatives by allocating resources, setting clear objectives, and championing data-driven practices at all levels of the organization. Leaders should actively promote a culture that values data-driven decision-making, ensuring that all departments understand the importance of leveraging data for strategic goals. Regularly communicating the benefits of data-driven strategies and celebrating data-driven successes can reinforce this commitment. Leaders must also provide the necessary tools, training, and technology to support data initiatives, showing a tangible investment in the organization's data capabilities.

Talent Acquisition and Development

Invest in talent acquisition and development initiatives to build a team of data scientists, analysts, and domain experts with the skills and expertise needed to drive data-driven innovation. This involves creating robust hiring processes to attract top talent and offering competitive salaries and benefits. Provide opportunities for training, mentorship, and career development to empower employees to succeed in data-driven roles. Encourage continuous learning through workshops, courses, and conferences, ensuring that the team stays updated on the latest trends and technologies in data science. Building a collaborative environment where knowledge sharing is encouraged can also enhance overall team capability.

Measure Impact and ROI

Establish metrics and key performance indicators (KPIs) to measure the impact and return on investment (ROI) of data-driven initiatives. Identify specific, quantifiable goals that align with strategic objectives, such as increased revenue, improved customer satisfaction, or reduced operational costs. Track progress against these metrics consistently, using dashboards and reports to visualize performance. Quantify the value generated by data-driven solutions by comparing pre- and post-implementation results. Communicate these results to stakeholders to demonstrate the business impact of data-driven decision-making, securing ongoing support and investment for future initiatives.

Continuous Improvement

Foster a culture of continuous improvement by soliciting feedback, learning from successes and failures, and adapting strategies based on insights gained from data-driven initiatives. Encourage a mindset where employees feel comfortable experimenting with innovative ideas and approaches without fear of failure. Implement mechanisms for regular review and iteration of data-driven projects, such as feedback loops and retrospective meetings. Celebrate achievements and analyze setbacks to identify areas for improvement. By promoting a culture of agility and innovation, organizations can adapt to changing environments and maintain a competitive edge in a rapidly evolving landscape.

USING ANALYTICS: CASE STUDIES IN DATA-DRIVEN SUCCESS

This section focuses on using analytics with case studies in data-driven success, highlighting their efficacy in addressing complex challenges and driving informed decision-making, including:

Industry-Specific Case Studies

Explore industry-specific case studies to understand how analytics can drive success in various sectors. By analyzing successful use cases in industries such as retail, healthcare, finance, and technology, organizations can gain insights into how analytics can be applied to address specific challenges, capitalize on opportunities, and achieve strategic objectives within their respective industries.

Lessons Learned

Extract valuable lessons learned from case studies to inform analytics strategies and initiatives. By identifying common themes, challenges, and success factors across different case studies, organizations can learn from others' experiences and apply best practices to optimize their own analytics projects, mitigate risks, and maximize impact.

Best Practices

Identify and adopt best practices derived from case studies to guide the implementation of analytics initiatives. By incorporating proven strategies, methodologies, and techniques into analytics projects, organizations can enhance the effectiveness and efficiency of their data-driven approaches, drive innovation, and achieve sustainable success in their analytics endeavors.

CASE STUDY COMPILATION: LESSONS FROM INDUSTRY-SPECIFIC DATA SUCCESSES

In the final module of our journey, let us review a comprehensive compilation of industry-specific case studies that highlight the transformative power of data-driven approaches across various sectors. These detailed examples extract valuable lessons learned and best practices that organizations can apply to drive success in their own data initiatives. By examining these real-world applications, we gain insights into how data-driven strategies can revolutionize operations, enhance decision-making, and create competitive advantages. Each case study provides a blueprint for leveraging data effectively, highlighting innovative solutions and measurable outcomes that can inspire and guide other organizations in their pursuit of data excellence.

Industry-Specific Case Studies

A collection of industry-specific case studies.

Retail: Dynamic Pricing Strategy

A leading retailer leveraged data analytics to implement dynamic pricing strategies, optimizing pricing in real-time based on demand, competition, and customer behavior. By analyzing historical sales data, customer purchasing patterns, and competitor pricing, the retailer developed algorithms that adjusted prices dynamically throughout the day. This approach allowed the retailer to offer competitive prices during peak demand periods while maximizing profit margins during slower times. Additionally, the data-driven pricing strategy enabled personalized discounts and promotions tailored to individual customer preferences, enhancing the shopping experience and driving customer loyalty. The implementation of dynamic pricing resulted in a significant increase in sales and profitability, demonstrating the power of data analytics in retail operations.

Healthcare: Predictive Analytics for Patient Care

A large hospital facility utilized predictive analytics to identify high-risk patients and intervene proactively, reducing hospital readmissions and improving patient outcomes. By integrating electronic health records (EHR), demographic data, and clinical indicators, the hospital developed predictive models that identified patients at risk of complications or readmission. These models enabled healthcare providers to tailor interventions and care plans to individual patient needs, ensuring timely and appropriate treatments. For example, high-risk patients received additional follow-up appointments, medication adjustments, and personalized discharge plans. The use of predictive analytics not only improved patient health outcomes but also optimized resource allocation and reduced healthcare costs by preventing avoidable readmissions and complications.

Finance: Personalized Investment Recommendations

A major financial institution employed machine learning algorithms to analyze customer preferences and risk profiles, delivering personalized investment recommendations that enhanced customer satisfaction and loyalty. By leveraging vast amounts of data from customer transactions, financial histories, and market trends, the institution developed sophisticated models that provided tailored investment advice. These recommendations were customized to align with individual financial goals, risk tolerance, and market conditions. The personalized approach helped clients make informed investment decisions, resulting in higher returns and reduced risks. Additionally, the institution's initiative-taking engagement with clients fostered trust and loyalty, positioning it as a leader in customer-centric financial services.

Technology: Predictive Maintenance in Manufacturing

A technology manufacturer implemented predictive maintenance strategies using IoT sensors and data analytics, reducing downtime and optimizing equipment performance in manufacturing facilities. By deploying sensors on critical machinery, the manufacturer collected real-time data on equipment conditions, such as temperature, vibration, and pressure. Advanced analytics and machine learning algorithms analyzed this data to predict potential failures and maintenance needs. As a result, maintenance could be scheduled proactively, preventing unexpected breakdowns and minimizing production disruptions. The predictive maintenance approach improved equipment lifespan, reduced maintenance costs, and enhanced overall operational efficiency. This data-driven strategy demonstrated the significant impact of predictive analytics on manufacturing performance and reliability.

Lessons Learned and Best Practices

A summary of lessons learned and best practices across case studies.

Invest in Data Infrastructure

Establishing a robust data infrastructure is crucial for ensuring the quality, security, and accessibility of data across the organization. This involves implementing reliable data storage solutions, such as data lakes or data warehouses, which can efficiently manage large volumes of structured and unstructured data. Additionally, setting up a comprehensive data governance framework is essential to maintaining data integrity and consistency. This framework should include policies and procedures for data management, data quality standards, data security measures, and access controls. By investing in advanced data infrastructure and governance, organizations can ensure that their data assets are dependable, secure, and readily available for analysis and decision-making, driving better business outcomes.

Foster Data Literacy

Promoting a culture of data literacy and continuous learning empowers employees to effectively leverage data in their roles. This involves offering training programs, workshops, and resources that cover essential data skills such as data interpretation, visualization, statistical analysis, and data ethics. Encouraging employees to participate in data-related projects and cross-functional teams can also enhance their practical experience and understanding of data-driven approaches. Furthermore, creating a supportive environment where employees feel comfortable asking questions and sharing knowledge is key to fostering data literacy. By investing in the development of data skills, organizations can build a workforce that can make informed decisions based on data insights, leading to improved performance and innovation.

Prioritize Ethical Considerations

Embedding ethical considerations into data initiatives is essential to ensuring fairness, transparency, and compliance with legal and regulatory requirements. This involves developing and enforcing policies that protect individuals' privacy, obtain informed consent, and uphold data security. Organizations should conduct regular ethical impact assessments to identify potential biases and mitigate risks in data collection, analysis, and decision-making processes. Additionally, fostering a culture of ethical awareness and accountability through training and clear communication helps employees understand the importance of ethical practices. By prioritizing ethics in data initiatives, organizations can build trust with stakeholders, avoid legal pitfalls, and ensure that their data-driven decisions are responsible and just.

Embrace Collaboration

Fostering cross-functional collaboration and communication is vital for breaking down silos and driving alignment on data-driven objectives and initiatives. Encouraging teamwork between departments such as IT, data science, marketing, and operations ensures that diverse perspectives are considered in data projects. Establishing regular meetings, collaborative platforms, and shared goals can enhance communication and coordination among teams. By promoting a collaborative culture, organizations can leverage the collective expertise and insights of their employees, leading to more innovative solutions and effective data-driven strategies. Collaboration also helps in identifying and addressing challenges more efficiently, contributing to the success of data initiatives.

Iterate and Adapt

Embracing a culture of experimentation and iteration allows organizations to continuously refine their data models and strategies based on feedback and insights gained from data analysis. This approach involves testing hypotheses, experimenting with different analytical methods, and learning from both successes and failures. Encouraging a mindset of continuous improvement helps organizations stay agile and responsive to changing business environments. Regularly reviewing and updating data models, processes, and technologies ensures that they remain relevant and effective. By iterating and adapting, organizations can optimize their data-driven approaches, enhance decision-making, and maintain a competitive edge in their industry.

Through these detailed case studies and best practices, organizations can glean valuable insights and inspiration to embark on their own data-driven journeys. By learning from real-world examples, they can better understand the practical applications and benefits of data-driven strategies. This knowledge empowers them to drive innovation, optimize operations, and achieve success in their respective industries. These examples serve as a roadmap, illustrating how data can be leveraged to solve complex problems, improve decision-making, and create competitive advantages. By embracing these practices, organizations can foster a culture of continuous improvement and adaptability in a rapidly evolving technological landscape.

IMPLEMENTATION ROADMAP: CASE STUDIES IN DATA-DRIVEN SUCCESS

This implementation roadmap outlines a comprehensive, step-by-step process for applying the case study approaches presented in this chapter in practice. This roadmap serves as a practical guide, providing clear, detailed instructions on how to collect, analyze, and interpret data to drive informed decision-making. By following this roadmap, organizations can systematically implement data-driven strategies, ensuring that they effectively harness the power of data analytics to achieve their objectives. This structured approach promotes consistency, accuracy, and efficiency in leveraging data insights, leading to better business outcomes and enhanced competitive advantage.

Roadmap Steps

- *Step 1*: Identify relevant industries, research case studies, and analyze key success factors.
- *Step 2*: Extract key insights, identify common patterns, and document lessons learned.
- *Step 3*: Develop best practices guidelines, share best practices internally, and incorporate best practices into strategy.

Step 1: Identify Relevant Industries, Research Case Studies, and Analyze Key Success Factors

Step 1 kickstarts the journey by pinpointing industries where data-driven approaches have thrived, researching case studies to uncover successful initiatives aligning with your organization's goals, and analyzing key success factors to inform the development of tailored strategies.

Identify Relevant Industries

Identify industries that are relevant to your organization or sector, focusing on those where data-driven approaches have demonstrated significant success. Consider industries with similar challenges or opportunities and analyze how they have leveraged data to drive innovation, efficiency, and growth. This identification process helps to ensure that the insights and strategies gleaned are applicable and can be adapted to your specific organizational context.

Research Case Studies

Conduct comprehensive research to gather industry-specific case studies that highlight successful data-driven initiatives. Focus on examples that align with your organization's goals and challenges, paying close attention to the methodologies employed, the data utilized, and the outcomes achieved. By thoroughly examining these case studies, you can gain a deeper understanding of how data-driven strategies are implemented and what factors contribute to their success.

Analyze Key Success Factors

Analyze the key success factors and strategies highlighted in each case study, identifying common themes, challenges, and best practices that can be applied to your own data-driven initiatives. Look for patterns in the data collection methods, analytical techniques, and implementation strategies that led to successful outcomes. By understanding these critical elements, you can adapt and tailor these best practices to fit your organization's unique needs and objectives, enhancing the likelihood of achieving similar successes.

Step 2: Extract Key Insights, Identify Common Patterns, and Document Lessons Learned

Step 2 is about extracting valuable insights from case studies, pinpointing common patterns and challenges, and documenting lessons learned to provide actionable recommendations for your organization's data-driven journey.

Extract Key Insights

Extract key insights and lessons learned from the case studies, focusing on strategies, methodologies, and approaches that have proven effective in driving data-driven success. Pay attention to the specific techniques and technologies used, as well as the organizational changes that facilitated successful implementation, and how these can be adapted to your context.

Identify Common Patterns

Identify common patterns, challenges, and success factors across multiple case studies, synthesizing them into actionable recommendations for your organization. Look for recurring themes such as effective data integration, stakeholder engagement, and iterative development processes, and consider how these patterns can inform your strategies.

Document Lessons Learned

Document the lessons learned from the case studies in a structured format, creating a repository of best practices and insights that can be shared with relevant stakeholders. This repository should be accessible and organized to facilitate easy reference and application, ensuring that the insights are leveraged to guide future data-driven initiatives effectively.

Step 3: Develop Best Practices Guidelines, Share Best Practices Internally, and Incorporate Best Practices into Strategy

Step 3 is about translating insights into action by developing guidelines based on case study findings, sharing them internally to promote knowledge exchange, and embedding these best practices into your organization's data strategy for informed decision-making and future initiatives.

Develop Best Practices Guidelines

Develop best practices guidelines based on the insights gleaned from the case studies, outlining recommended approaches, methodologies, and strategies for implementing data-driven initiatives. These guidelines should cover a range of topics, including data collection, analysis, and visualization techniques, as well as ethical considerations and governance frameworks. Additionally, provide specific examples and case study references to illustrate the application of these best practices in real-world scenarios. Ensure that the guidelines are detailed, practical, and tailored to the unique needs and context of your organization, making them a valuable resource for teams embarking on data-driven projects.

Share Best Practices Internally

Share the best practices guidelines internally within your organization, disseminating knowledge and insights to relevant teams and departments. Utilize various communication channels, such as internal newsletters, workshops, training sessions, and online collaboration platforms, to ensure widespread awareness and understanding of the guidelines. Encourage open discussions and feedback sessions to address any questions or concerns and to refine the guidelines further. By actively promoting and sharing these best practices, you can foster a culture of continuous learning and improvement where teams are equipped with the knowledge and tools needed to succeed in their data-driven endeavors.

Incorporate Best Practices into Strategy

Incorporate the best practices into your organization's data strategy and planning processes, ensuring that lessons learned from case studies are applied to future data-driven initiatives. Integrate these guidelines into strategic planning documents, project management frameworks, and performance evaluation metrics. Encourage leaders and decision-makers to prioritize and adhere to these best practices when defining project goals, allocating resources, and assessing project outcomes. By embedding these practices into the core of your data strategy, you can create a structured approach that promotes consistency, efficiency, and effectiveness across all data-driven projects. This strategic integration will help your organization leverage data more effectively to achieve its objectives and drive innovation.

By following this implementation roadmap, organizations can leverage industry-specific case studies to extract valuable insights, lessons learned, and best practices. This comprehensive approach enables organizations to apply proven strategies and methodologies to their own data-driven initiatives, tailored to their unique contexts and challenges. As a result, organizations can drive success, enhance decision-making processes, and foster innovation by learning from the experiences of others. Implementing these insights helps to avoid common pitfalls, optimize resources, and achieve strategic objectives, leading to improved performance and competitive advantage in their respective industries.

CONCLUSION

By examining various case studies, best practices, and practical implementation strategies, this module has equipped readers with the knowledge and tools to harness the power of data effectively. Whether it is through enhancing operational efficiency, optimizing customer experiences, or driving innovation, the insights gained from this comprehensive guide will empower decision-makers to leverage data for informed decision-making and sustainable growth. As organizations continue to navigate an increasingly data-centric world, the principles and strategies outlined in this book will serve as a foundation for building resilient, agile, and competitive enterprises.

## CHAPTER 8

THE FUTURE OF DATA ANALYTICS

D ata analytics is entering an era of unprecedented transformation. As new technologies continue to emerge and mature, the capabilities of data analytics are rapidly expanding, enabling organizations to derive deeper insights, make faster decisions, and adapt more readily to changing markets. This chapter explores the exciting future of data analytics, examining how developments in artificial intelligence (AI), real-time processing, data privacy, and advanced visualization are reshaping the field. We'll delve into how these advancements will impact industries, drive innovation, and provide actionable insights for organizations looking to harness the full potential of data.

The future of data analytics promises a shift from traditional, retrospective analysis to real-time, predictive, and prescriptive analytics. This evolution will help organizations not only understand past trends but also forecast future ones and make proactive decisions based on these insights. As companies leverage data for competitive advantage, data analytics is expected to be fully embedded in decision-making processes, influencing every department from operations to marketing.

EMERGING TRENDS SHAPING THE FUTURE OF DATA ANALYTICS

Several major trends are driving the evolution of data analytics. These include advanced AI, edge computing, augmented analytics, automated machine learning (AutoML), and the increasing importance of data ethics and privacy. Each of these trends has the potential to redefine how data is collected, processed, and used to drive decision-making.

Advanced AI and Machine Learning (ML)

AI, particularly machine learning (ML), is enhancing data analytics in unprecedented ways. Future analytics platforms will increasingly incorporate

AI-driven insights that automate and accelerate data analysis. ML algorithms can detect patterns within data that would be impossible for humans to identify, enabling organizations to extract predictive insights, streamline operations, and personalize customer experiences.

In particular, deep learning—a subset of ML that models complex patterns in data—will likely play a larger role in the analytics landscape. For example, neural networks can analyze unstructured data such as images, videos, and natural language, allowing organizations to gain insights from a wider range of data sources. With advancements in AI and ML, analytics will move beyond mere pattern recognition to develop prescriptive analytics, recommending specific actions based on predictions.

Real-Time Analytics and Edge Computing

The demand for real-time data insights is growing across industries, as organizations seek to make faster and more agile decisions. Traditional data analytics has typically relied on batch processing, where data is collected and analyzed periodically. The future, however, will see a shift toward real-time analytics, where data is processed and analyzed as it is generated. This shift is largely driven by advances in edge computing, which enables data to be processed closer to its source rather than sending it back to centralized data centers.

Edge computing allows for faster processing speeds, reduced latency, and increased data security, making it ideal for time-sensitive applications like financial trading, autonomous vehicles, and industrial automation. By integrating edge computing with analytics, organizations can respond to events instantly, providing a significant competitive advantage in fast-paced industries. The ability to analyze data at the edge will allow businesses to derive insights and take action in milliseconds, transforming how decisions are made.

Augmented Analytics

Augmented analytics refers to the use of AI to enhance data analytics processes by automating data preparation, insight generation, and insight explanation. This trend is democratizing analytics, enabling employees without technical expertise to leverage data for decision-making. By automating routine aspects of data analysis, augmented analytics tools allow analysts and business users to focus on interpreting insights and developing strategic responses.

One major aspect of augmented analytics is natural language processing (NLP), which enables users to interact with data through natural language queries, much like asking a question in everyday conversation. For example, a manager could type or speak a query like "What were the sales trends last quarter?" and receive an answer in seconds. This technology empowers individuals at all levels of an organization to leverage data, reducing the dependence on specialized data teams and enabling faster, more informed decisions.

Automated Machine Learning (AutoML)

AutoML is revolutionizing the way ML models are created, evaluated, and deployed. AutoML automates key stages of the ML pipeline, including feature selection, model selection, and hyperparameter tuning. This automation makes ML accessible to a broader audience, including business analysts and decision-makers without a background in data science.

As AutoML tools become more advanced, we can expect to see wider adoption of predictive analytics across organizations. AutoML platforms allow users to build models faster and more efficiently, removing many of the traditional barriers to ML adoption. By automating complex processes, AutoML democratizes ML and enables organizations to harness predictive analytics without requiring extensive data science expertise.

Data Ethics, Privacy, and Governance

As organizations increasingly rely on data to drive decision-making, ethical considerations surrounding data collection, privacy, and usage are coming to the forefront. In response to high-profile data breaches and the misuse of personal information, new regulations such as the General Data Protection Regulation (GDPR) in Europe and the California Consumer Privacy Act (CCPA) in the U.S. are being enacted to protect consumers' rights.

The future of data analytics will require companies to prioritize data ethics and privacy, adopting governance frameworks that ensure transparency, accountability, and responsible data use. Organizations will need to integrate privacy-preserving techniques, such as differential privacy and federated learning, into their analytics workflows. These techniques allow companies to analyze data without compromising individual privacy, balancing the need for insights with respect for user rights.

In addition, ethical considerations will extend to how AI models are trained and used, ensuring that they do not reinforce biases or make unfair decisions. As data becomes more central to organizational strategies, establishing a culture of ethical data usage will be essential for maintaining trust with consumers and stakeholders.

TECHNOLOGICAL ADVANCEMENTS IMPACTING DATA ANALYTICS

The future of data analytics will be shaped by advancements in several technologies. Here's a look at some of the most impactful developments that are poised to transform data analytics.

Quantum Computing

Quantum computing is on the horizon as a revolutionary force in data analytics. Quantum computers have the potential to perform calculations at speeds far beyond what is possible with classical computers, making them ideal for analyzing extremely large datasets. With quantum computing, tasks that would take classical computers years to complete could potentially be solved in seconds, opening up new possibilities for big data analysis and complex modeling.

While quantum computing is still in its early stages, advancements in this field could one day enable organizations to analyze massive datasets in real time, solve optimization problems faster, and develop more sophisticated ML models. Companies are already exploring the potential of quantum computing to address challenges in finance, healthcare, logistics, and other data-intensive industries.

Blockchain Technology for Data Integrity

Blockchain technology is emerging as a solution to issues of data integrity and transparency. In a blockchain, data is stored in a decentralized, tamper-proof ledger, ensuring that once data is entered, it cannot be altered. This makes blockchain ideal for industries that require stringent data integrity, such as finance, healthcare, and supply chain management.

By integrating blockchain with data analytics, organizations can ensure the accuracy and reliability of their data, as every transaction and data point is verified and recorded. Blockchain also enables enhanced traceability, allowing organizations to track the origin and history of data, which can be particularly useful in complex data ecosystems involving multiple stakeholders.

Advanced Data Visualization Tools

As data becomes more complex, the ability to visualize it effectively is essential for understanding and communication. Future analytics platforms will include advanced data visualization tools that go beyond traditional charts and graphs. Immersive visualization technologies, such as augmented reality (AR) and virtual reality (VR), will allow users to interact with data in three-dimensional environments, providing new perspectives and insights.

AR and VR can be particularly useful in scenarios where spatial data is relevant, such as logistics, urban planning, or environmental monitoring. By visualizing data in 3D, users can better understand complex relationships, identify trends, and make more informed decisions.

Internet of Things (IoT) and Connected Devices

The Internet of Things (IoT) is rapidly expanding, with billions of connected devices generating data every second. As IoT adoption increases, data analytics will play a critical role in analyzing this vast amount of information. IoT devices provide real-time data from various sources, such as industrial machinery, vehicles, and wearable devices, which can be analyzed to optimize operations, predict equipment failures, and improve customer experiences.

In the future, IoT analytics will become more integrated, enabling organizations to analyze data from multiple sources simultaneously and derive insights that span different systems. This will enable more holistic decision-making, where analytics considers factors from across an entire ecosystem, rather than focusing on isolated data points.

The Evolution of Data-Driven Decision Making

As data analytics capabilities evolve, the nature of decision-making itself is changing. In the past, decision-making was often based on historical data and gut instinct. The future of data analytics, however, will enable predictive and prescriptive analytics, where decisions are guided by real-time data and forecasts of future events.

For instance, predictive analytics can forecast trends and project outcomes based on existing patterns, allowing businesses to anticipate changes and proactively adjust their strategies. Prescriptive analytics goes a step further, recommending specific actions based on predictions, thus optimizing decision-making processes. This evolution represents a shift from reactive to proactive decision-making, where businesses anticipate changes and respond before they happen.

CONCLUSION

The future of data analytics holds enormous potential, defined by groundbreaking technological advancements, increased accessibility for users of all skill levels, and a stronger focus on ethical considerations and governance. These developments collectively promise to transform data analytics from a niche function within organizations to a core strategic asset driving decision-making across industries. As new technologies such as AI, ML, edge computing, and quantum computing mature, data analytics will move beyond descriptive and diagnostic analyses toward predictive and prescriptive insights, enabling organizations to not only understand what has happened but also to anticipate what is likely to happen and recommend optimal courses of action.

Embracing Technological Advancements for a Competitive Edge

Organizations that proactively adopt and integrate these emerging technologies will find themselves in a favorable position to maintain a competitive edge in an increasingly data-driven world. Technological innovations, such as real-time data processing, AutoML, and augmented analytics, are simplifying data processes and opening the door for individuals at all organizational levels to harness the power of data. Advanced AI models, enhanced ML algorithms, and sophisticated visualization techniques are reducing the need for specialized data skills, allowing decision-makers to generate and interpret insights more independently. With these advancements, data analytics is becoming more inclusive, enabling employees from various departments to make data-backed decisions and contribute meaningfully to an organization's growth and innovation.

The Role of Ethics and Data Governance in the Future of Analytics

As data collection, storage, and analysis capabilities grow, so too does the responsibility to manage data ethically and transparently. Ethical considerations are no longer optional but have become a fundamental part of how organizations approach data analytics. Consumers and stakeholders are increasingly aware of and concerned with how their data is used. The future of data analytics will demand that organizations commit to responsible data practices that prioritize user privacy, fairness, and accountability. Transparent data governance frameworks, rooted in regulatory standards such as GDPR and CCPA, will be essential for building trust with customers and ensuring compliance with evolving laws. Implementing responsible data governance practices will enable organizations to manage data more effectively, mitigate risks, and avoid potential reputational damage associated with unethical data usage.

Data as a Strategic Asset

Data has become one of the most valuable assets an organization possesses, and as analytics capabilities evolve, this value will only increase. By treating data as a strategic asset, businesses can use it to uncover hidden patterns, streamline operations, reduce costs, and foster innovation. In the future, data analytics will not only support business strategies but drive them. Executives and managers will rely on data insights to guide product development, customer engagement, supply chain management, and financial planning. Strategic decisions that were once based on intuition and historical data will increasingly be informed by predictive and real-time data, enabling organizations to adapt dynamically to market changes, consumer preferences, and global trends.

Building a Data-Driven Culture

To fully realize the benefits of data analytics, organizations must foster a data-driven culture, encouraging employees at all levels to engage with data and recognize its importance. This involves not only providing the necessary tools and training but also embedding data analytics into the decision-making processes and workflows of every department. A data-driven culture empowers employees to take ownership of data initiatives, making data a central part of daily operations, rather than a back-office function. Such a culture encourages experimentation, innovation, and continuous improvement, ultimately contributing to an organization's resilience and adaptability in a fast-changing business landscape. By making data analytics accessible to a wider range of users and providing support for developing data literacy, organizations can create an environment where data is trusted, insights are valued, and decision-making is consistently improved.

Anticipating the Challenges and Preparing for the Future

While the future of data analytics is promising, it is not without its challenges. Rapid technological advancements and the proliferation of data sources create complexities in data management, integration, and security. Organizations will need to invest in infrastructure, talent, and tools that support scalable data solutions. Additionally, with the increase in AI and ML applications, there is a growing need for transparency and interpretability in analytics models. As models become more complex, ensuring that insights are understandable and actionable for all stakeholders becomes paramount. By anticipating these challenges and proactively developing solutions, organizations can be better prepared to adapt to the evolving data landscape and sustain long-term growth and success.

Toward a Future Where Data is Central to Every Industry

As we look forward, it is clear that data analytics will become an indispensable element across all industries, from healthcare and finance to retail and manufacturing. In healthcare, data analytics will enable more personalized and preventive care, allowing providers to anticipate patient needs and intervene earlier. In finance, real-time analytics will enhance fraud detection, optimize investment strategies, and improve customer satisfaction. Retailers will use analytics to personalize the shopping experience, optimize inventory, and adapt to shifting consumer behaviors. Manufacturing will benefit from predictive maintenance, optimizing production schedules and reducing downtime. The versatility and applicability of data analytics mean that its impact will be felt in virtually every sector, transforming traditional business models and unlocking new revenue streams.

Empowering Decision-Makers with Data-Driven Insights

At its core, data analytics is about empowering decision-makers to make better, faster, and more informed choices. The future of data analytics will be characterized by an ability to access and analyze data in real time, enabling business leaders to respond swiftly to emerging trends and challenges. With augmented analytics, decision-makers without technical expertise will be able to interact with data through natural language queries, making data insights more accessible and actionable. The move toward democratizing analytics means that data-driven insights will no longer be confined to specialized teams but will be available to all employees, encouraging a more agile and informed approach to decision-making. By bridging the gap between data and decision-making, analytics will become a vital tool for navigating uncertainty and driving sustainable growth.

Data Analytics as a Path to Innovation and Growth

In summary, the future of data analytics is a promising one, filled with opportunities for technological innovation, strategic growth, and enhanced decision-making. As organizations invest in advanced analytics tools and build data-driven cultures, they position themselves to leverage data as a catalyst for innovation. The trends discussed in this chapter illustrate a future where data analytics is integral to every aspect of business, fostering more informed, ethical, and agile decision-making processes. With data analytics, organizations can transform raw data into valuable insights, creating a pathway to a more innovative, resilient, and competitive future. By embracing the possibilities that data analytics offers, businesses will not only adapt to a changing world but also shape it.

## CHAPTER 9

GETTING STARTED WITH DATA ANALYTICS DEVELOPMENT

I n today's data-centric world, the ability to analyze data effectively is a crucial skill for business leaders, strategists, and decision-makers. This chapter provides a comprehensive introduction to setting up a productive data analytics development environment. A solid foundation is essential to enable efficient data processing, visualization, and analysis, equipping you with the tools necessary to turn raw data into actionable insights. This chapter walks you through the essential steps for building an environment that supports all aspects of data analytics, from data preparation to advanced visualization and modeling, using Python and its extensive suite of data-focused libraries.

By learning how to set up a reliable environment tailored to your specific needs, you'll gain the skills required to maximize efficiency and productivity when working with data. Whether you are performing descriptive analysis, designing visualizations, or building predictive models, having a well-designed development setup empowers you to experiment confidently and adapt to new challenges within the data analytics space.

SETTING UP A DATA ANALYTICS DEVELOPMENT ENVIRONMENT

The development environment is the foundation of all data work. In data analytics, a good environment supports smooth data manipulation, visualization, and model building without imposing technical bottlenecks. This involves selecting the right software, configuring essential libraries, and potentially choosing hardware that can handle larger datasets and complex operations. Setting up Python, along with popular integrated development environments (IDEs) such as Jupyter Notebook or Visual Studio Code (VS Code), allows for flexibility and supports a range of tasks that are essential in the field of data analytics.

Choosing and Installing Python as the Primary Language

Python is the most widely used programming language for data analytics due to its readability, extensive library support, and strong community that fosters knowledge-sharing. It's a language designed for simplicity, making it accessible for those with minimal programming experience while still powerful enough for complex tasks. Installing Python involves downloading the latest version from the official Python Web site (*https://www.python.org/downloads/*). Ensure that you select Add Python to PATH during installation to make it accessible from any command line or terminal.

Once installed, you can leverage Python's rich ecosystem to handle various data tasks. Python serves as a central tool in data analytics, supporting functions for data cleaning, transformation, visualization, and statistical analysis. With Python as the primary language, data analysts have access to a wide array of libraries tailored to nearly every need, making Python an indispensable part of the analytics workflow.

Selecting the Right IDE

A powerful IDE facilitates the efficient coding, testing, and debugging of scripts and provides tools for data visualization and workflow management. For data analytics, Jupyter Notebook is one of the most popular IDEs, allowing for an interactive coding experience where you can view code outputs in real time, making it ideal for exploratory data analysis. Jupyter Notebook is particularly valuable for producing reports, as it combines code, text, and visualizations in one interface, simplifying the communication of insights.

VS Code is another strong option, especially for projects that involve extensive code development, such as building larger models or integrating with other tools. VS Code's extensions allow you to customize your environment to include syntax highlighting, real-time debugging, and access to multiple programming languages. Choosing an IDE depends on the needs of your project; Jupyter Notebook is excellent for analysis and visualization, while VS Code is well suited for more comprehensive projects.

Hardware Considerations for Data Processing

The hardware requirements for data analytics vary depending on the complexity and size of the datasets being analyzed. Basic analytics, such as descriptive statistics or small-scale visualizations, can be comfortably handled on a standard laptop or desktop. Larger datasets and complex models, however, such as machine learning algorithms, can benefit from a machine with higher RAM and a multi-core processor. Graphics processing units (GPUs), while not essential for traditional analytics, become advantageous when working on high-performance data tasks such as deep learning or image processing. Understanding your hardware needs allows you to plan for future growth as your data analytics projects become more advanced.

INTRODUCTION TO PYTHON FOR DATA ANALYTICS

Python is at the heart of modern data analytics, valued for its simplicity, adaptability, and vast selection of libraries that streamline complex data tasks. For those new to Python, it is essential to start with the language's basics, including variables, data structures, and fundamental operations. Python's versatility means that it's widely used for everything from basic data cleaning to complex statistical modeling.

In the context of data analytics, some key areas to focus on when learning Python include:

- *Data structures*: Lists, dictionaries, and tuples are core components that allow for flexible data storage and manipulation.
- *Control structures*: `if-else` statements, loops, and functions enable you to create scripts that process data iteratively and conditionally.
- *Library importing and management*: Python's libraries, such as pandas, NumPy, and Matplotlib, play a pivotal role in data analytics. Understanding how to import, configure, and use these libraries effectively is crucial for performing efficient data operations.

The strength of Python in data analytics lies not only in the language itself but also in the extensive libraries that enable you to execute a variety of tasks with ease.

Essential Libraries for Data Analytics

Python's utility in data analytics is greatly expanded by libraries that add powerful functions for data manipulation, statistical analysis, and visualization:

- *pandas*: pandas is the backbone of data manipulation in Python, featuring powerful tools for organizing, filtering, aggregating, and cleaning data. It provides the DataFrame structure, which allows for spreadsheet-like data organization but with greater flexibility and functionality. With pandas, you can quickly load data from various sources, clean and transform it, and perform analysis using intuitive commands.
- *NumPy*: NumPy is crucial for numerical operations and is widely used in tasks that involve arrays and matrix operations. It provides functions for generating random numbers, performing mathematical operations, and handling multidimensional data arrays. NumPy's efficiency and speed make it especially valuable for handling large datasets, and it serves as a foundation for other libraries, including pandas and scikit-learn.
- *Matplotlib and Seaborn*: Visualization is key to understanding data, and Matplotlib is Python's foundational library for creating plots, charts, and graphs. Seaborn, built on Matplotlib, simplifies creating attractive statistical visualizations and is particularly useful for producing heatmaps,

box plots, and other complex visualizations. Both libraries help analysts to visualize patterns and trends within data, facilitating the interpretation and communication of results.

• *Scikit-learn*: For those interested in predictive analytics, scikit-learn offers a suite of machine learning tools for tasks such as regression, classification, and clustering. Although more commonly associated with machine learning, scikit-learn is increasingly used in advanced analytics due to its accessible API and a variety of preprocessing functions that simplify data preparation.

Each of these libraries has unique features, and by learning to harness them, analysts can approach data from multiple angles, extracting maximum value through sophisticated manipulations and insights.

PRACTICAL APPLICATION: SETTING UP A DATA ANALYTICS ENVIRONMENT AND RUNNING AN INITIAL ANALYSIS

Setting up a data analytics environment can seem daunting at first, but by following these steps, you'll be ready to run your first data analysis in no time. Let's walk through a simple setup using Python and Jupyter Notebook, a powerful combination for data analysis.

Step-by-Step Guide to Setting Up and Running an Analysis

1. Download and install Python:
   • Begin by visiting the Python Web site (*https://www.python.org/downloads/*) and downloading the latest version.
   • During installation, ensure you select Add Python to PATH to streamline access from the command line.
2. Install Jupyter Notebook:
   • Open a terminal or command prompt.
   • Use `pip install notebook` to install Jupyter Notebook, which will serve as the primary IDE for data analysis in this guide.
3. Set up a virtual environment (optional but recommended):
   • Virtual environments help manage dependencies for specific projects, ensuring that you can work with the exact versions of libraries needed.
   • Create one by running `python -m venv myenv` in the terminal, replacing `myenv` with your preferred environment name.
   • Activate the environment and install the necessary libraries within it.
4. Install core libraries:
   • While in your virtual environment, install pandas, NumPy, and Matplotlib by running `pip install pandas numpy matplotlib`. These libraries are essential for data manipulation and visualization.

5. Run a basic data analysis script:

- Open Jupyter Notebook by typing `jupyter notebook` in the terminal. This will launch Jupyter in your default Web browser.
- In Jupyter, create a new notebook and start by importing pandas, NumPy, and Matplotlib.
- Write a small script to load a dataset, clean it, and generate a simple visualization. For instance, use pandas to load a CSV file, check for missing values, and plot a bar chart with Matplotlib.

Example Script: Loading and Visualizing Data

To demonstrate the setup, consider a script that loads a dataset, performs basic cleaning, and visualizes trends:

```
import pandas as pd
import numpy as np
import matplotlib.pyplot as plt
 Load data
data = pd.read_csv('sample_data.csv')
 Data cleaning
data = data.dropna()   Remove missing values
 Basic analysis
average_value = data['Value'].mean()
 Visualization
plt.figure(figsize=(10,6))
plt.hist(data['Value'], bins=20)
plt.title('Value Distribution')
plt.xlabel('Value')
plt.ylabel('Frequency')
plt.show()
```

This example script covers essential tasks: loading data, cleaning it, calculating a summary statistic, and visualizing the data distribution. By following this process, you gain experience with the basic workflow in data analytics, laying the groundwork for more advanced analyses in future projects.

CONCLUSION

This chapter provided the necessary guidance to set up a robust development environment for data analytics. By understanding Python basics, configuring essential libraries, and setting up a workspace tailored to analytics, you have gained a strong foundational understanding. With this setup, aspiring data analysts can approach projects with a clear strategy, performing efficient data manipulations, generating insightful visualizations, and eventually exploring more advanced topics, such as predictive analytics. By mastering these fundamental skills, you will be well prepared to turn data into actionable insights and contribute meaningfully to data-driven decision-making in any organization.

GLOSSARY OF KEY TERMS

This glossary provides definitions and explanations of key concepts and terms commonly encountered in the field of data science and decision-making

A

A/B testing: A statistical method used to compare two versions of a variable (e.g., a Web page) to determine which performs better. Frequently used in marketing and product optimization.

Accuracy: The ratio of correctly predicted instances to the total instances in a classification task, measuring overall model performance.

Active learning: A machine learning approach where the model interactively queries users to label specific data points, improving the model's accuracy with fewer labeled instances.

Adaptive Boosting (AdaBoost): A boosting algorithm that combines multiple weak learners to form a stronger classifier, adjusting the weights based on prior model errors.

Adjusted R-squared: A modified version of R-squared in regression analysis that accounts for the number of predictors, indicating the proportion of variance explained by the model.

Aggregated data: Data summarized from more granular to higher levels to identify trends and patterns.

Algorithm: A sequence of steps or rules designed to perform a specific task. Algorithms form the basis of machine learning models for analyzing data and making predictions.

Anomaly detection: Techniques to identify data points or patterns that significantly differ from the rest of the dataset, often used in fraud detection and quality control.

Application programming interface (API): A set of protocols allowing different software applications to communicate. Critical for integrating machine learning models into applications.

Artificial intelligence (AI): Machines or software mimicking human cognitive functions such as learning, problem-solving, and perception. Foundational to fields such as machine learning.

Association rule learning: A technique in data mining to find interesting relationships or associations between variables, commonly used in market basket analysis.

Autoencoder: A type of neural network in unsupervised learning that encodes data into a lower dimension and then decodes it. Often used in anomaly detection and data compression.

B

Bayesian inference: The process of updating the probability of a hypothesis as new evidence is observed. Often used in probabilistic modeling.

Bayesian statistics: A statistical approach using Bayes' theorem to update probabilities with new data. Widely applied in predictive modeling.

Bias: A systematic error in data collection or models leading to inaccurate predictions. Can result from sample selection, data quality, or model assumptions.

Big data: Extremely large datasets characterized by volume, velocity, and variety, requiring specialized tools for processing and analysis.

Binary classification: Classification with two possible classes, such as spam/not spam. Common binary classifiers include logistic regression and support vector machines.

Bootstrap aggregating (Bagging): An ensemble technique where multiple models are trained on random subsets of the data, with their predictions averaged to improve accuracy.

C

Categorical data: Data representing discrete groups or categories, often needing encoding for machine learning models.

Class imbalance: A scenario in classification tasks where one class significantly outnumbers the other, requiring techniques such as resampling to improve model performance.

Classification: A machine learning task where data is assigned predefined labels. Examples include logistic regression, decision trees, and neural networks.

Clustering: An unsupervised learning method that groups similar data points based on their features. Algorithms include k-means, DBSCAN, and hierarchical clustering.

Cohen's kappa: A metric to evaluate agreement between observed and predicted classifications, accounting for chance agreement.

Confusion matrix: A matrix to evaluate classification performance by showing actual versus predicted values across classes. Used to calculate accuracy, precision, recall, and F1-score.

Correlation: A statistical measure of how two variables move in relation to each other, with positive, negative, or no correlation.

Cross-entropy loss: A loss function in classification that measures the difference between predicted and actual probability distributions.

Cross-validation: A method to evaluate model performance by dividing data into training and testing sets multiple times, reducing overfitting.

Curse of dimensionality: The phenomenon where higher dimensions make data more sparse, complicating model training.

D

Data augmentation: Creating new training examples from existing data. Commonly used in image data to improve model generalization.

Data engineering: The design, construction, and maintenance of data pipelines and infrastructure essential for data analysis and modeling.

Data governance: Policies and practices ensuring data quality, security, and compliance across an organization.

Data lake: A storage system that holds raw data in its native format, allowing diverse types of data for processing as needed.

Data mining: The process of discovering patterns in large datasets, using methods such as association, clustering, and classification.

Data normalization: Scaling data to a common range without distorting differences in value distribution. Essential for machine learning models.

Data science: An interdisciplinary field focused on extracting insights and knowledge from data using scientific and computational methods.

Decision boundary: In classification, the line or surface that separates classes in feature space.

Decision tree: A model that splits data into branches based on feature values. Commonly used for classification and regression tasks.

Deep learning: A machine learning subset with neural networks featuring many layers. Widely applied in image and language processing.

Dimensionality reduction: Uses techniques such as PCA to reduce the number of features, improving model efficiency and performance.

Dropout: A regularization method in neural networks that randomly omits units during training, reducing overfitting.

Dynamic time warping: A method to measure similarity between temporal sequences that may vary in time. Often applied in time-series analysis.

E

Early stopping: A regularization technique to prevent overfitting by halting training when validation performance declines.

Elastic Net: A regression model with L1 and L2 penalties, balancing feature selection and stability.

Ensemble learning: Combining predictions from multiple models to improve overall performance, using methods such as bagging and boosting.

Exploratory data analysis (EDA): The process of analyzing and visualizing data to summarize main characteristics and guide further analysis.

Exponential smoothing: A time-series forecasting method that weighs recent data points more heavily than older ones.

F

F1-score: The harmonic mean of precision and recall. Useful for evaluating classification models on imbalanced datasets.

Feature engineering: Creating new features from raw data to improve model performance, such as aggregations or transformations.

Feature importance: A technique that ranks features based on their predictive value in a model, aiding in feature selection.

Feature scaling: Standardizing feature ranges for consistent model perfor-mance, using techniques such as normalization and standardization.

Feature selection: Identifying relevant features that improve model accuracy while reducing complexity.

G

Generalization: The ability of a model to perform well on new, unseen data, indicating it has not overfitted to the training data.

Gradient boosting: An ensemble technique that sequentially builds models to correct the errors of previous models. Popular in high-performance applications.

Gradient descent: An optimization algorithm that adjusts model parameters to minimize the cost function iteratively.

Grid search: An exhaustive search for hyperparameter tuning by testing all possible combinations within a specified grid.

H

Hierarchical clustering: A clustering method that builds a tree-like structure of clusters, either merging or splitting data iteratively.

Holdout set: A subset of data set aside for final model testing, ensuring unbiased evaluation.

Hyperparameter tuning: The process of optimizing hyperparameters to improve model performance, often using techniques such as grid search or random search.

I

Imbalanced data: When classes in a classification problem have unequal representation, affecting model accuracy.

Instance-based learning: A learning approach where the model memorizes examples rather than learning an explicit representation, such as k-nearest neighbors.

K

K-fold cross-validation: A technique to assess model performance by splitting data into k parts, training on k−1, and testing on the remaining part, repeating for all partitions.

K-means clustering: A popular clustering algorithm that assigns data points to k clusters based on proximity to centroids.

L

L1 regularization (Lasso): A regularization technique that adds an L1 penalty to the cost function, encouraging sparsity in the model by setting irrelevant features to 0.

L2 regularization (Ridge): A technique that adds an L2 penalty to the cost function to prevent overfitting by limiting model complexity.

Latent variable: An unobserved variable inferred from the observed data, often used in factor analysis and dimensionality reduction.

M

Mean absolute error (MAE): A measure of prediction error in regression, averaging absolute differences between predictions and actual values.

Model drift: When a model's performance degrades over time due to changes in the data distribution, requiring model retraining.

N

Natural language processing (NLP): The field within AI focused on enabling machines to understand, interpret, and generate human language.

Neural network: A computational model mimicking the brain's neuron structure. Fundamental to deep learning applications.

O

Overfitting: When a model captures noise in the training data rather than the true pattern, resulting in poor generalization to new data.

P

Precision: The proportion of true positives among all positive predictions in classification. Important for understanding model accuracy.

Principal component analysis (PCA): A dimensionality reduction method that transforms data into a new coordinate system with maximized variance.

This glossary serves as a reference for understanding key terms and concepts in the field of data science and decision-making. It provides a foundation for further exploration and learning in this rapidly evolving and interdisciplinary field.

ETHICAL CONSIDERATIONS FRAMEWORK

OVERVIEW

This framework provides a comprehensive framework equipped with guidelines, methodologies, and tools tailored to address these challenges. By adopting a proactive approach to ethics, decision-makers can navigate complex ethical landscapes, uphold integrity, and foster trust in data-driven decision-making processes.

FRAMEWORK

Establishing Ethical Foundations

- *Ethical Principles in Data Science*: Define core ethical principles, including transparency, fairness, accountability, privacy, and respect for individual rights. These principles serve as foundational pillars guiding ethical conduct throughout the data science lifecycle.
- *Ethical Decision-Making Framework*: Introduce a systematic approach to ethical decision-making encompassing key steps such as ethical issue identification, stakeholder analysis, impact assessment, and mitigation planning.
- *Ethical Risk Assessment*: Conduct a thorough ethical risk assessment to identify potential ethical risks and vulnerabilities associated with data science initiatives.

Privacy Preservation

- *Privacy Risk Management*: Implement privacy risk management practices to identify, assess, and mitigate privacy risks associated with data collection, storage, processing, and sharing.
- *Privacy-Enhancing Technologies*: Explore techniques such as data anonymization, encryption, differential privacy, and homomorphic

encryption to enhance privacy protections while maintaining data utility.

- *Regulatory Compliance*: Ensure compliance with relevant privacy regulations and standards, such as GDPR, CCPA, HIPAA, and sector-specific regulations governing the handling of sensitive data.

Mitigating Bias and Ensuring Fairness

- *Bias Identification and Mitigation*: Develop methodologies for identifying, measuring, and mitigating bias in data and algorithms, ensuring fair and equitable outcomes across diverse demographic groups.
- *Algorithmic Fairness*: Implement fairness-aware machine learning techniques and fairness metrics to address algorithmic biases and promote fairness in decision-making processes.
- *Ethical Data Sampling and Representation*: Address biases in data sampling and representation to ensure that datasets accurately reflect the diversity of populations and avoid perpetuating historical biases.

Transparency and Accountability

- *Transparency in Decision-Making*: Foster transparency by documenting data sources, methodologies, assumptions, and limitations in data science projects, enabling stakeholders to understand and scrutinize decision-making processes.
- *Accountability Mechanisms*: Establish accountability mechanisms such as audit trails, access controls, and governance structures to hold individuals and organizations accountable for their actions and decisions in data-driven contexts.
- *Ethical Communication*: Communicate findings, insights, and uncertainties transparently and accurately to stakeholders, avoiding misleading interpretations or misrepresentations of data-driven results.

Ethical AI Development and Deployment

- *Ethical AI Principles*: Define ethical principles for AI development and deployment, emphasizing values such as human-centered design, safety, fairness, transparency, and accountability.
- *Ethical AI Governance*: Establish governance frameworks, oversight mechanisms, and ethical review boards to ensure responsible AI development, deployment, and monitoring.
- *Human Oversight and Control*: Maintain human oversight and control over AI systems, enabling human intervention to correct errors, mitigate biases, and ensure ethical decision-making in critical contexts.

Cultural and Societal Impacts

- *Cultural Awareness and Sensitivity*: Promote cultural awareness and sensitivity among data science practitioners to recognize and address cultural biases, values, and norms that may influence ethical decision-making.

- *Community Engagement and Collaboration*: Engage with diverse communities and stakeholders to solicit input, feedback, and co-creation of data-driven solutions that align with community values and priorities.
- *Social Responsibility*: Foster a culture of social responsibility within organizations and the broader data science community, advocating for ethical practices, transparency, and accountability in data-driven endeavors.

CONCLUSION

- *Continuous Ethical Reflection*: Emphasize the importance of continuous ethical reflection, learning, and adaptation to evolving ethical standards, societal expectations, and technological advancements in data science.
- *Ethical Leadership*: Encourage ethical leadership and responsibility among decision-makers, practitioners, and organizations to champion ethical conduct, integrity, and trustworthiness in data-driven decision-making processes.

PYTHON CODE FILES

CHAPTER 1 EXAMPLE

```python
import pandas as pd
import seaborn as sns
import matplotlib.pyplot as plt

# Data setup
data_1 = {
"Date": ["4/1/2024", "4/1/2024", "4/1/2024", "4/1/2024",
"4/2/2024", "4/2/2024", "4/2/2024", "4/2/2024"],
"Store": ["Store A", "Store A", "Store B", "Store B",
"Store A", "Store A", "Store B", "Store B"],
"Product ID": ["ABC123", "XYZ456", "ABC123", "XYZ456",
"ABC123", "XYZ456", "ABC123", "XYZ456"],
"Sales QTY": [50, 30, 40, 25, 60, 35, 45, 28],
"Inventory Level": [200, 150, 180, 120, 140, 115, 135, 92]
}

df_1 = pd.DataFrame(data_1)
# Visualization 1: Sales Quantity by Store and Date
plt.figure(figsize=(10, 6))
sns.lineplot(data=df_1, x='Date', y='Sales QTY',
hue='Store', style='Store', markers=True, dashes=False)
plt.title('Sales Quantity by Store and Date')
plt.show()

# Visualization 2: Inventory Levels by Store and Date
plt.figure(figsize=(10, 6))
sns.lineplot(data=df_1, x='Date', y='Inventory Level',
hue='Store', style='Store', markers=True, dashes=False)
plt.title('Inventory Levels by Store and Date')
plt.show()
```

Code Explanation

This code demonstrates basic data manipulation and visualization in Python, using pandas for handling data and Seaborn and matplotlib.pyplot for plotting. It begins by setting up a sample dataset, representing daily sales and inventory levels for products in two stores, organized in columns such as Date, Store, Product ID, Sales QTY, and Inventory Level. The dataset is then converted into a DataFrame for easy analysis. In the first visualization, a line plot shows Sales QTY by Date for each store, with Seaborn distinguishing stores by color and marker style. The second visualization follows the same structure to plot Inventory Level by Date, offering a quick comparison of inventory trends across stores. These visualizations provide insights into daily sales and inventory fluctuations, which is valuable for tracking store performance over time.

CHAPTER 2 EXAMPLE

```
import pandas as pd
import seaborn as sns
import matplotlib.pyplot as plt

# Data setup
data_2 = {
"Timestamp": ["8:00 AM", "8:15 AM", "8:30 AM", "8:45 AM",
"9:00 AM", "9:15 AM", "9:30 AM"],
"Temperature (°C)": [75, 76, 77, 78, 80, 82, 83],
"Vibration (mm/s)": [12.5, 12.6, 12.7, 12.8, 13.0, 13.2,
13.3],
"Pressure (psi)": [100, 102, 105, 107, 110, 112, 115],
"Failure": [0, 0, 0, 0, 0, 1, 1]
}

df_2 = pd.DataFrame(data_2)

# Visualization: Temperature, Vibration, Pressure Trends
plt.figure(figsize=(12, 7))
sns.lineplot(data=df_2, x='Timestamp', y='Temperature
(°C)', label='Temperature (°C)', color='red')
sns.lineplot(data=df_2, x='Timestamp', y='Vibration
(mm/s)', label='Vibration (mm/s)', color='blue')
sns.lineplot(data=df_2, x='Timestamp', y='Pressure (psi)',
label='Pressure (psi)', color='green')
plt.title('Equipment Monitoring: Temp, Vibration, and
Pressure')
plt.legend()
plt.show()
```

Code Explanation

This code snippet sets up and visualizes equipment monitoring data using Python. First, it imports pandas for data handling, and Seaborn and matplotlib.pyplot for plotting. The data dictionary, data_2, includes timestamped readings of `Temperature` (°C), `Vibration` (mm/s), `Pressure` (psi), and an indicator column, `Failure`, with values indicating normal operation (0) and failure (1). The data is then converted to a pandas DataFrame for structured analysis. A line plot is created to show trends for temperature, vibration, and pressure over time, with Seaborn used to plot each variable in a different color (red for temperature, blue for vibration, and green for pressure). The plot provides a visual summary of the equipment's operational data over the selected time period, which helps in identifying trends or warning signs preceding equipment failure.

CHAPTER 3 EXAMPLE

```
import pandas as pd
import seaborn as sns
import matplotlib.pyplot as plt

# Data setup
data_3 = {
"Date": ["1/1/2024", "1/1/2024", "1/1/2024", "1/1/2024",
"1/1/2024", "1/1/2024"],
"Region": ["East", "East", "East", "West", "West", "West"],
"Product Category": ["Electronics", "Apparel", "Home
Goods", "Electronics", "Apparel", "Home Goods"], "Revenue
(USD)": [15000, 10000, 12000, 18000, 9000, 11000],
"Market Share (%)": [20, 15, 18, 25, 12, 16], "Trend":
["Growing", "Stable", "Declining", "Growing", "Stable",
"Declining"]
}

df_3 = pd.DataFrame(data_3)

# Visualization: Revenue by Product Category and Region
plt.figure(figsize=(10, 6))
sns.barplot(data=df_3, x='Product Category', y='Revenue
(USD)', hue='Region')
plt.title('Revenue by Product Category and Region')
plt.show()
```

Code Explanation

This code visualizes regional revenue data by product category, using pandas for data handling and Seaborn and matplotlib.pyplot for plotting. It first sets up `data_3`, a dictionary capturing revenue-related information, including `Date`, `Region`, `Product Category`, `Revenue (USD)`, `Market Share (%)`, and `Trend` for various product categories in two regions (`East` and `West`). This data is then converted into a DataFrame for analysis. The visualization uses `sns.barplot` to display `Revenue (USD)` on the y axis, categorized by `Product Category` on the x axis and differentiated by `Region` using color. The bar chart gives a clear comparison of revenue for each product category across regions, helping to identify which categories perform best in each area.

CHAPTER 4 EXAMPLE

```
import pandas as pd
import seaborn as sns
import matplotlib.pyplot as plt

# Data setup
data_4 = {
"Customer ID": ["001", "002", "003", "004", "005", "006"],
"Product ID": ["ABC123", "XYZ456", "LMN789", "ABC123",
"PQR789", "XYZ456"], "Category": ["Electronics", "Apparel",
"Home Goods", "Electronics", "Electronics", "Apparel"],
"Price (USD)": [500, 50, 100, 500, 300, 60], "Purchase
Date": ["2024-01-01", "2024-01-01", "2024-01-01",
"2024-01-02", "2024-01-02", "2024-01-02"]
}

df_4 = pd.DataFrame(data_4)

# Visualization: Sales Volume by Product Category
plt.figure(figsize=(8, 5))
sns.countplot(x='Category', data=df_4)
plt.title('Sales Volume by Product Category')
plt.show()
```

Code Explanation

This code creates a visualization of sales volume by product category. It begins by setting up a dataset, `data_4`, which includes fields such as `Customer ID`, `Product ID`, `Category`, `Price (USD)`, and `Purchase Date`, simulating product purchases across different categories (`Electronics`, `Apparel`, and `Home Goods`). This dataset is converted into a pandas DataFrame for easy analysis. The visualization uses `sns.countplot` to show the count of purchases by `Category` on the *x* axis, which reflects the sales volume per category. Displayed as a bar chart, this plot quickly reveals the popularity of each category based on purchase frequency, helping identify high-demand product types.

CHAPTER 5 EXAMPLE

```
import pandas as pd
import seaborn as sns
import matplotlib.pyplot as plt

# Data setup
data_5 = {
"Customer ID": ["001", "002", "003", "004", "005", "006"],
"Age": [35, 45, 28, 55, 40, 30], "Gender": ["Male",
"Female", "Male", "Male", "Female", "Male"], "Income
(USD)": [50000, 60000, 40000, 70000, 55000, 48000], "Loan
Amount (USD)": [10000, 20000, 15000, 30000, 18000, 12000],
"Loan Approval": ["Approved", "Approved", "Denied",
"Approved", "Denied", "Approved"]
}
```

```
df_5 = pd.DataFrame(data_5)

# Visualization: Loan Approval Rates by Gender
plt.figure(figsize=(8, 5))
sns.countplot(x='Gender', hue='Loan Approval', data=df_5)
plt.title('Loan Approval Rates by Gender')
plt.show()
```

Code Explanation

This code creates a visualization of loan approval rates by gender. It begins by setting up a dataset, `data_5`, which contains fields such as `Customer ID`, `Age`, `Gender`, `Income (USD)`, `Loan Amount (USD)`, and `Loan Approval`. This sample data is then converted into a pandas DataFrame for analysis. The visualization employs `sns.countplot` to display counts of loan approvals and denials for each gender. The `hue='Loan Approval'` argument differentiates `Approved` and `Denied` loan statuses with color. This bar chart effectively shows loan approval rates between genders, helping identify any trends or disparities in loan approval outcomes.

CHAPTER 6 EXAMPLE

```
import pandas as pd
import seaborn as sns
import matplotlib.pyplot as plt

# Data setup
data_6 = {
"Date": ["1/1/2024", "1/1/2024", "1/1/2024", "1/2/2024",
"1/2/2024", "1/2/2024"], "Department": ["Cardiology",
"Pediatrics", "Emergency", "Surgery", "Obstetrics",
"Oncology"], "Patient ID": ["001", "002", "003", "004",
"005", "006"], "Diagnosis": ["Coronary Artery Disease",
"Pneumonia", "Fractured Arm", "Appendicitis", "Normal
Delivery", "Breast Cancer"],  "Treatment": ["Angioplasty",
"Antibiotics", "Casting", "Appendectomy", "NA",
"Chemotherapy"],  "Length of Stay": [3, 5, 1, 2, 1, 10],
"Outcome": ["Successful", "Recovered", "Discharged",
"Successful", "Discharged", "Ongoing Care"]
}

df_6 = pd.DataFrame(data_6)

# Visualization: Length of Stay by Department
plt.figure(figsize=(10, 6))
sns.boxplot(x='Department', y='Length of Stay', data=df_6)
plt.title('Length of Stay by Department')
plt.show()
```

Code Explanation

This code creates a visualization of patient length of stay by department in a healthcare setting. It starts by defining a sample dataset, `data_6`, which includes `Date`, `Department`, `Patient ID`, `Diagnosis`, `Treatment`, `Length of Stay`, and `Outcome`. This data is then converted into a pandas DataFrame for structured analysis. The visualization uses `sns.boxplot` to plot `Length of Stay` on the y axis, grouped by `Department` on the x axis. This box plot displays the spread of patient stay durations within each department, highlighting the median, quartiles, and any potential outliers. Such a visualization aids in understanding the typical patient stay lengths by department, potentially guiding resource allocation and patient flow management in healthcare.

DATASETS

BUSINESS SALES AND MARKETING

Overview: This dataset includes information on product sales and marketing spend by region and quarter. It contains fields for Product, Region, Quarter, Sales Revenue, and Marketing Spend.

Use cases:

- *Sales analysis*: Readers can analyze sales performance by product, region, and quarter to identify trends and key drivers of revenue.
- *ROI calculation*: Use sales and marketing spend data to calculate the return on investment (ROI) for different products and marketing strategies.
- *Segmentation*: Segment regions or products based on sales to better understand customer demand.

Product	Region	Quarter	Sales Revenue	Marketing Spend
Product B	South	Q4	30168	6539
Product B	East	Q3	34338	11217
Product C	West	Q2	42411	16308
Product C	West	Q2	44700	10925
Product B	North	Q4	34204	19189
Product A	North	Q2	10459	5387
Product A	South	Q3	24479	18481
Product B	South	Q4	39796	7198
Product B	North	Q1	10531	8667

Product	Region	Quarter	Sales Revenue	Marketing Spend
Product B	West	Q2	35531	8075
Product C	East	Q1	34801	14538
Product B	South	Q4	29865	18483
Product C	North	Q1	11015	9024
Product C	West	Q1	15710	19110
Product A	South	Q1	32393	19103
Product B	South	Q1	48771	10125
Product C	West	Q2	12051	8313
Product A	West	Q2	32907	16696
Product A	East	Q4	25510	13947
Product B	North	Q4	35845	18191
Product C	South	Q2	36765	7885
Product A	South	Q4	48450	8925
Product A	East	Q3	18277	8060
Product A	South	Q3	37907	11601
Product B	North	Q2	21458	17142
Product A	East	Q1	49514	6917
Product A	South	Q3	24023	14648
Product A	East	Q3	14193	18196
Product B	North	Q3	33740	8305
Product A	North	Q1	25385	12291
Product B	West	Q4	22235	6773
Product B	North	Q3	22799	10717
Product C	West	Q2	42509	17044
Product C	South	Q1	39479	5714
Product B	North	Q4	15624	9430
Product B	West	Q1	31041	18816
Product B	West	Q4	41988	15295
Product B	East	Q4	25635	15470
Product A	South	Q4	22468	15289
Product B	West	Q1	39790	14727
Product C	East	Q1	11939	6249
Product A	West	Q4	31892	8615
Product C	West	Q1	29201	8104

Product	Region	Quarter	Sales Revenue	Marketing Spend
Product C	West	Q3	42722	19089
Product A	North	Q3	39629	17888
Product C	North	Q2	22263	8840
Product A	North	Q3	18335	13176
Product A	South	Q2	24099	9093
Product A	West	Q1	18038	14816
Product B	South	Q1	42977	10403
Product C	South	Q4	13960	5057
Product A	West	Q4	41883	17471
Product A	South	Q3	25307	8154
Product C	South	Q2	47567	7846
Product B	North	Q3	37793	13731
Product A	South	Q3	46415	5872
Product C	South	Q2	22497	17304
Product B	East	Q2	22620	6370
Product B	East	Q4	27875	17431
Product B	West	Q3	26730	12169
Product A	East	Q1	12672	5052
Product A	South	Q4	45732	13175
Product B	North	Q4	17850	11969
Product A	West	Q4	34032	13911
Product B	South	Q4	23704	5175
Product A	East	Q4	27057	11104
Product C	West	Q1	32459	7611
Product B	South	Q4	34375	17181
Product A	West	Q3	26009	5712
Product C	North	Q1	26589	12150
Product A	West	Q2	24185	12211
Product C	West	Q4	37886	9114
Product C	South	Q3	43746	14021
Product B	West	Q3	38071	17275
Product B	North	Q2	20307	19402
Product B	South	Q3	37497	19231
Product A	East	Q1	44243	8113

Product	Region	Quarter	Sales Revenue	Marketing Spend
Product A	South	Q4	17661	13011
Product B	West	Q3	37087	14303
Product B	North	Q3	15294	9084
Product A	East	Q4	32625	15555
Product B	West	Q3	36806	8314
Product B	East	Q1	38261	6973
Product C	North	Q3	46525	8563
Product B	West	Q3	16077	11616
Product A	South	Q1	21931	5635
Product B	South	Q2	31662	7602
Product B	East	Q2	46735	12281
Product B	North	Q3	23981	15832
Product B	East	Q3	31603	13325
Product A	North	Q1	42771	10491
Product A	West	Q1	46735	18282
Product B	West	Q2	15561	14064
Product C	West	Q4	48455	5262
Product B	West	Q4	11095	13956
Product C	East	Q4	34531	14177
Product C	South	Q4	26023	7656
Product B	East	Q4	21632	18369
Product C	East	Q4	43496	12487
Product A	West	Q2	45547	11852

RETAIL TRANSACTIONS

Overview: This dataset simulates transactions in a retail setting, with fields such as Transaction ID, Date, Customer ID, Product Category, and Amount Spent.

Use cases:

- *Customer behavior analysis*: Track spending habits by analyzing transaction amounts and product categories.
- *Seasonal trends*: Use transaction dates to identify seasonal spending trends, helping readers understand how demand varies over time.
- *Exploratory data analysis (EDA)*: Practice data wrangling and visualization techniques to gain insights into customer purchasing patterns.

Store ID	Year	Revenue Growth	Customer Satisfaction	Productivity Index
1	2023	0.1	9	85.9
2	2022	0.06	5	67.57
3	2023	0.19	8	94.44
4	2021	0.2	8	67.07
5	2021	0.05	3	55.87
6	2022	0.12	9	52.37
7	2023	0.08	6	75.05
8	2021	0.06	9	92.66
9	2022	0.17	6	94.14
10	2021	0.06	9	68.48
11	2021	0.18	1	77.12
12	2023	0.18	9	80.4
13	2021	0.07	8	95.91
14	2023	0.02	1	50.18
15	2021	0.14	6	71.95
16	2021	0.17	6	59.91
17	2021	0.06	6	82.46
18	2023	0.12	7	76.45
19	2023	0.12	5	51.66
20	2021	0.07	6	53.29
21	2022	0.12	4	80.75
22	2021	0.12	1	91.88
23	2021	0.15	1	83.79
24	2022	0.05	1	92.65
25	2023	0.02	7	51.57
26	2022	0.02	1	61.41
27	2021	0.14	9	76.81
28	2021	0.08	6	74.71
29	2022	0.06	2	75.64
30	2021	0.07	8	87.99
31	2022	0.2	7	70.94
32	2021	0.1	7	59.63
33	2022	0.16	5	92.9

Store ID	Year	Revenue Growth	Customer Satisfaction	Productivity Index
34	2022	0.04	1	81.11
35	2022	0.04	5	71.76
36	2023	0.05	2	64.48
37	2022	0.08	8	96.21
38	2023	0.05	2	93.39
39	2023	0.18	7	52.56
40	2021	0.08	6	72.73
41	2022	0.14	2	61.66
42	2022	0.18	5	64.77
43	2022	0.11	8	85.27
44	2021	0.13	1	87.12
45	2022	0.13	2	96.07
46	2021	0.19	6	68.6
47	2021	0.13	7	78.03
48	2023	0.06	2	62.71
49	2023	0.17	7	87.55
50	2021	0.12	1	60.74
51	2023	0.03	3	77.62
52	2022	0.14	7	76.96
53	2022	0.18	3	64.41
54	2021	0.09	7	69.26
55	2023	0.17	8	92.29
56	2023	0.16	6	86.13
57	2022	0.05	2	86.19
58	2021	0.03	8	74.44
59	2022	0.13	4	76.31
60	2023	0.19	7	60.44
61	2022	0.17	1	62.26
62	2023	0.01	1	89.64
63	2022	0.05	6	93.93
64	2023	0.03	3	80.56
65	2023	0.19	8	98.61
66	2023	0.05	5	50.67
67	2021	0.07	1	97.99

Store ID	Year	Revenue Growth	Customer Satisfaction	Productivity Index
68	2021	0.08	3	92.38
69	2023	0.09	8	55.16
70	2021	0.11	5	75.8
71	2023	0.14	1	97.96
72	2021	0.05	4	90.11
73	2023	0.1	9	65.15
74	2021	0.01	5	80.97
75	2023	0.11	3	92.14
76	2021	0.09	6	57.45
77	2021	0.13	2	88.79
78	2021	0.11	9	96.88
79	2021	0.11	9	75.24
80	2023	0.1	4	57.98
81	2023	0.18	2	63.74
82	2021	0.08	2	60.05
83	2023	0.12	1	59.72
84	2023	0.15	6	50.05
85	2021	0.13	7	59.22
86	2021	0.11	8	57.98
87	2022	0.03	8	67.78
88	2022	0.09	6	57.48
89	2021	0.15	1	60.77
90	2021	0.08	6	94.97
91	2023	0.09	7	72.32
92	2023	0.14	4	64.29
93	2021	0.16	5	77.22
94	2023	0.04	3	52.36
95	2021	0.04	1	98.89
96	2023	0.07	5	88.5
97	2023	0.18	5	65.99
98	2023	0.04	2	71.79
99	2022	0.07	9	87.78
100	2022	0.17	9	94.41

CITY POLLUTION LEVELS

Overview: This dataset contains daily pollution levels for different cities, along with temperature and population density. Fields include `City`, `Date`, `Pollution Level`, `Temperature`, and `Population Density`.

Use cases:

- *Environmental trends*: Visualize pollution levels over time to identify potential causes and seasonal fluctuations.
- *Correlation analysis*: Analyze relationships between temperature, population density, and pollution levels.
- *Forecasting*: Apply time-series analysis techniques to predict future pollution levels based on past data.

City	Date	Pollution Level	Temperature	Population Density
City D	1/1/2023	253	26.28	4776
City D	1/2/2023	220	15.01	3022
City B	1/3/2023	148	21.92	1021
City C	1/4/2023	138	25.81	3139
City B	1/5/2023	82	20.13	2564
City D	1/6/2023	104	23.28	3098
City B	1/7/2023	154	28.04	3291
City D	1/8/2023	90	26.7	3696
City B	1/9/2023	81	18.14	3324
City C	1/10/2023	72	16.39	4313
City A	1/11/2023	151	17.22	4131
City A	1/12/2023	237	21.04	1827
City D	1/13/2023	71	28.05	3301
City D	1/14/2023	80	15.16	4199
City C	1/15/2023	290	21.65	2315
City B	1/16/2023	264	19.25	2447
City D	1/17/2023	244	15.83	2978
City B	1/18/2023	89	16.56	2152
City B	1/19/2023	233	15.06	2629
City C	1/20/2023	58	25.4	2218
City C	1/21/2023	99	15.02	2588
City B	1/22/2023	231	16.06	3095

City	Date	Pollution Level	Temperature	Population Density
City B	1/23/2023	172	16.93	3831
City D	1/24/2023	123	27.28	3604
City D	1/25/2023	246	18.63	3768
City A	1/26/2023	50	16.62	4174
City B	1/27/2023	273	16.07	2112
City B	1/28/2023	228	15.35	1767
City A	1/29/2023	278	23.98	1840
City A	1/30/2023	278	19.3	3504
City C	1/31/2023	98	21.78	3434
City C	2/1/2023	116	22.16	4941
City D	2/2/2023	161	21.26	2278
City B	2/3/2023	231	29.1	4622
City D	2/4/2023	137	28.85	3423
City C	2/5/2023	196	18	1414
City C	2/6/2023	292	26.67	2943
City B	2/7/2023	236	17.12	1321
City C	2/8/2023	83	23.51	1907
City C	2/9/2023	119	22.67	3767
City D	2/10/2023	238	18.79	2706
City A	2/11/2023	263	17.12	4237
City A	2/12/2023	210	18.66	2773
City D	2/13/2023	174	29.05	4669
City B	2/14/2023	180	23.76	4193
City A	2/15/2023	138	16.79	3368
City B	2/16/2023	65	18.54	4957
City D	2/17/2023	57	27.39	2858
City A	2/18/2023	73	16.7	4266
City B	2/19/2023	285	28.62	3740
City A	2/20/2023	112	27.99	3223
City B	2/21/2023	294	24.27	4349
City B	2/22/2023	246	18.37	2731
City A	2/23/2023	55	21.52	2379
City B	2/24/2023	78	27.69	4099

City	Date	Pollution Level	Temperature	Population Density
City B	2/25/2023	150	20.73	4696
City D	2/26/2023	149	21.3	1515
City D	2/27/2023	202	21.78	4065
City C	2/28/2023	76	15.12	2854
City A	3/1/2023	232	17.21	4122
City A	3/2/2023	285	26.81	3588
City B	3/3/2023	209	21.15	2400
City B	3/4/2023	206	20.81	2508
City C	3/5/2023	59	25.86	4972
City B	3/6/2023	247	17.64	4043
City B	3/7/2023	81	21.5	4735
City D	3/8/2023	263	21.49	3356
City B	3/9/2023	165	23.46	1230
City A	3/10/2023	260	27.12	1620
City C	3/11/2023	196	25.49	1673
City D	3/12/2023	260	29.31	1151
City A	3/13/2023	221	18.55	4013
City D	3/14/2023	123	17.71	4160
City B	3/15/2023	230	21.02	1473
City B	3/16/2023	217	23.4	4937
City B	3/17/2023	265	22.61	1596
City C	3/18/2023	111	20	3855
City A	3/19/2023	179	27.66	3747
City B	3/20/2023	213	20.33	3655
City C	3/21/2023	204	16.51	4514
City B	3/22/2023	218	16.99	2395
City A	3/23/2023	194	15.79	2838
City D	3/24/2023	70	18.51	2372
City C	3/25/2023	130	29.87	3855
City C	3/26/2023	204	26.58	2672
City B	3/27/2023	191	24.8	1883
City B	3/28/2023	209	28.1	4873
City A	3/29/2023	245	23.61	4031

City	Date	Pollution Level	Temperature	Population Density
City C	3/30/2023	55	21.04	2112
City D	3/31/2023	275	29.36	1872
City D	4/1/2023	98	28.58	1372
City A	4/2/2023	198	27.1	4652
City C	4/3/2023	139	18.08	1576
City D	4/4/2023	62	23.09	4251
City C	4/5/2023	125	21.03	3735
City C	4/6/2023	267	21.88	2174
City B	4/7/2023	188	17.68	1530
City A	4/8/2023	176	17.01	1642
City A	4/9/2023	130	15.64	4527
City B	4/10/2023	87	23.45	1578

HOUSING PRICES

Overview: This dataset provides simulated data on housing sales, with features such as House ID, Location, Size (sq ft), Bedrooms, Bathrooms, and Sale Price.

Use cases:

- *Predictive modeling*: Use features such as house size, location, and number of bedrooms/bathrooms to predict sale prices using regression techniques.
- *Feature engineering*: Practice creating new features, such as price per square foot or bedroom-to-bathroom ratio, to improve model accuracy.
- *Data pre-processing*: Use data wrangling techniques to handle missing values, scale features, and prepare the data for modeling.

House ID	Location	Size (sq ft)	Bedrooms	Bathrooms	Sale Price
1	Urban	2672	2	2	382409
2	Suburban	2225	4	2	182072
3	Suburban	569	3	3	547205
4	Urban	1379	2	1	687103
5	Urban	962	3	2	348090
6	Urban	1282	4	1	164426
7	Urban	1212	1	3	506990

House ID	Location	Size (sq ft)	Bedrooms	Bathrooms	Sale Price
8	Suburban	676	4	2	240440
9	Rural	961	1	2	259472
10	Suburban	3034	4	2	182427
11	Urban	2267	2	2	404842
12	Suburban	709	2	3	689639
13	Rural	1978	3	3	333371
14	Urban	667	3	3	241945
15	Suburban	2782	1	2	570434
16	Rural	2615	3	1	623581
17	Rural	3840	2	1	767426
18	Suburban	1677	4	3	114781
19	Suburban	3403	1	1	243802
20	Suburban	2028	1	1	693658
21	Rural	1945	3	2	644879
22	Suburban	1646	3	3	141941
23	Urban	737	1	3	114624
24	Urban	3929	4	2	752968
25	Urban	1684	2	1	121266
26	Urban	3560	4	1	454751
27	Urban	3315	4	1	318982
28	Urban	3249	4	1	399779
29	Suburban	3283	1	3	517009
30	Suburban	2577	3	2	592322
31	Rural	2576	2	2	248130
32	Rural	2761	4	3	427573
33	Rural	2544	4	1	208759
34	Suburban	898	1	3	423851
35	Suburban	2125	2	2	265241
36	Urban	575	1	1	253227
37	Suburban	2306	3	1	413448
38	Rural	1070	4	2	590058
39	Suburban	1678	3	3	531414
40	Rural	3446	4	1	470035

House ID	Location	Size (sq ft)	Bedrooms	Bathrooms	Sale Price
41	Rural	2464	4	1	670566
42	Urban	1455	4	3	238296
43	Urban	3550	1	3	767123
44	Urban	3894	3	3	385379
45	Suburban	3094	1	3	724807
46	Urban	963	2	1	178636
47	Suburban	3052	3	3	694406
48	Rural	1876	1	3	606909
49	Suburban	1596	2	1	651928
50	Urban	3202	1	1	697105
51	Suburban	1120	3	2	483537
52	Urban	1890	4	3	586261
53	Suburban	1521	3	1	458397
54	Suburban	2046	1	3	367147
55	Rural	1832	3	1	122733
56	Suburban	1021	1	2	565684
57	Rural	3508	1	3	740686
58	Rural	1876	1	3	633132
59	Rural	2369	2	3	762220
60	Rural	739	4	2	792533
61	Rural	3449	1	1	218434
62	Suburban	2410	1	2	579725
63	Suburban	3548	4	1	148109
64	Urban	3594	1	1	728714
65	Urban	1460	3	1	459552
66	Rural	3592	1	3	719511
67	Suburban	2459	2	1	146205
68	Rural	2018	4	3	146892
69	Rural	3650	2	2	664228
70	Rural	654	3	2	365309
71	Urban	1283	3	3	659587
72	Urban	1832	4	2	453665
73	Rural	3698	2	2	732468

House ID	Location	Size (sq ft)	Bedrooms	Bathrooms	Sale Price
74	Rural	3505	4	1	272004
75	Urban	798	1	2	336871
76	Urban	1468	4	3	180710
77	Rural	2514	4	1	506003
78	Suburban	2955	1	3	592832
79	Suburban	3562	1	1	377111
80	Suburban	2383	4	2	250240
81	Suburban	2875	2	3	797726
82	Rural	1479	2	1	694440
83	Urban	1433	2	1	329009
84	Urban	688	4	3	288231
85	Urban	3959	1	2	161456
86	Urban	1254	2	2	569017
87	Suburban	1372	2	3	564935
88	Rural	3515	1	2	478076
89	Rural	918	3	2	778767
90	Urban	1467	4	1	177585
91	Rural	521	3	3	110147
92	Urban	2915	1	3	295847
93	Rural	2566	3	1	580335
94	Suburban	1974	3	1	348077
95	Suburban	3808	4	3	799788
96	Rural	2873	2	3	740139
97	Urban	3806	1	3	360656
98	Rural	3724	1	2	629594
99	Urban	514	2	3	307350
100	Urban	1254	3	3	156379

CREDIT RISK ASSESSMENT

Overview: This dataset includes records for credit applicants, with fields such as Applicant ID, Credit Score, Income, Loan Status, and Approval Decision.

Use cases:

- *Classification modeling*: Build a classification model to predict loan approval based on applicant attributes such as credit score and income.
- *Bias and fairness evaluation*: Assess potential biases in loan approvals. This is a useful exercise in understanding ethical considerations in predictive modeling.
- *Decision trees and logistic regression*: Use decision tree or logistic regression algorithms to predict loan status and assess the impact of features on credit approval.

Applicant ID	Credit Score	Income	Loan Status	Approval Decision
1	610	103029	Declined	No
2	546	43071	Declined	No
3	724	59120	Approved	No
4	378	36085	Declined	No
5	531	112261	Approved	No
6	501	102781	Approved	No
7	303	113380	Declined	No
8	366	62090	Approved	Yes
9	748	92047	Declined	Yes
10	781	32463	Approved	Yes
11	375	45840	Declined	No
12	584	49204	Approved	Yes
13	379	32855	Approved	Yes
14	310	88066	Declined	No
15	314	96355	Approved	Yes
16	770	50118	Declined	No
17	567	47810	Declined	No
18	533	48513	Declined	Yes
19	500	81554	Approved	No
20	457	86457	Approved	No
21	419	106893	Approved	No
22	747	41497	Declined	No
23	379	113763	Declined	Yes
24	499	73786	Declined	No

Applicant ID	Credit Score	Income	Loan Status	Approval Decision
25	446	104269	Declined	Yes
26	495	95504	Approved	Yes
27	429	113015	Approved	No
28	780	42156	Declined	Yes
29	361	100437	Approved	Yes
30	728	83185	Approved	No
31	418	66109	Approved	No
32	608	76055	Approved	No
33	638	106513	Declined	No
34	570	58809	Declined	No
35	652	85999	Approved	Yes
36	373	59215	Approved	No
37	376	119019	Approved	No
38	803	103395	Declined	Yes
39	452	81132	Declined	No
40	765	112290	Declined	Yes
41	700	114451	Approved	No
42	722	30876	Declined	No
43	805	112053	Declined	Yes
44	467	97929	Approved	No
45	505	90773	Approved	Yes
46	349	97402	Approved	Yes
47	324	47751	Declined	Yes
48	496	43151	Approved	No
49	310	43820	Declined	No
50	728	32592	Approved	Yes
51	463	117592	Approved	No
52	794	59274	Approved	No
53	357	112295	Declined	No
54	747	40609	Declined	Yes
55	732	83094	Approved	No
56	581	68432	Approved	No
57	643	109297	Declined	No

Applicant ID	Credit Score	Income	Loan Status	Approval Decision
58	538	61942	Approved	Yes
59	590	36427	Approved	No
60	733	71619	Approved	Yes
61	694	59472	Approved	Yes
62	519	72619	Approved	Yes
63	774	118793	Declined	Yes
64	393	118363	Approved	No
65	319	37709	Approved	Yes
66	448	109533	Declined	No
67	310	90508	Approved	No
68	623	56059	Declined	No
69	683	118462	Declined	Yes
70	413	81562	Approved	Yes
71	465	118507	Approved	Yes
72	542	95162	Approved	No
73	391	110560	Declined	Yes
74	345	82629	Approved	No
75	534	118336	Approved	No
76	519	112976	Approved	No
77	476	107048	Approved	Yes
78	833	103003	Approved	No
79	438	98265	Approved	Yes
80	825	37281	Approved	No
81	605	68642	Declined	No
82	552	87465	Declined	Yes
83	380	113416	Declined	No
84	588	65833	Declined	Yes
85	456	48783	Approved	No
86	371	48471	Declined	Yes
87	406	93769	Approved	No
88	411	113168	Approved	No
89	687	111518	Declined	No
90	595	91938	Approved	Yes

Applicant ID	Credit Score	Income	Loan Status	Approval Decision
91	312	100058	Declined	Yes
92	758	97553	Declined	Yes
93	678	112470	Approved	Yes
94	447	96347	Declined	Yes
95	727	38363	Approved	No
96	734	105326	Declined	No
97	406	101456	Approved	No
98	759	107813	Declined	Yes
99	613	111705	Declined	Yes
100	600	64873	Declined	No

EMPLOYEE ENGAGEMENT SURVEY

Overview: This dataset contains employee engagement scores, department information, satisfaction levels, and tenure. Fields include Employee ID, Department, Satisfaction Score, Engagement Score, and Tenure.

Use cases:

- *Engagement analysis*: Analyze trends in employee engagement across different departments and tenures.
- *Predictive analysis*: Identify factors that correlate with higher engagement or satisfaction, which can inform HR practices.
- *Clustering*: Use clustering techniques to group employees with similar engagement patterns, potentially identifying teams that may need targeted interventions.

Employee ID	Department	Satisfaction Score	Engagement Score	Tenure
1	HR	4	5	14
2	Engineering	6	5	12
3	Sales	7	8	18
4	Marketing	1	9	4
5	Sales	2	9	10
6	Sales	3	3	2
7	Engineering	4	3	14
8	Sales	3	2	12
9	HR	8	7	9

Employee ID	Department	Satisfaction Score	Engagement Score	Tenure
10	Sales	8	3	15
11	Engineering	3	1	12
12	Sales	4	4	13
13	Marketing	5	2	17
14	Marketing	5	6	6
15	Sales	5	2	9
16	Sales	9	6	2
17	Sales	7	8	18
18	Engineering	6	2	14
19	Marketing	4	3	19
20	Marketing	7	8	1
21	Marketing	1	5	18
22	Engineering	9	5	6
23	Marketing	6	2	14
24	Marketing	6	5	14
25	Marketing	1	2	4
26	Engineering	5	5	19
27	HR	6	1	16
28	Engineering	6	3	10
29	Marketing	8	2	18
30	Marketing	8	3	6
31	Sales	8	9	1
32	Marketing	8	7	14
33	Engineering	6	9	4
34	Sales	1	8	3
35	Engineering	8	8	11
36	Engineering	8	9	2
37	Marketing	9	4	2
38	HR	5	4	8
39	HR	9	1	17
40	Engineering	3	8	2
41	HR	3	5	4
42	Sales	2	8	3

Employee ID	Department	Satisfaction Score	Engagement Score	Tenure
43	Marketing	9	3	9
44	Marketing	8	3	17
45	Sales	7	8	16
46	HR	2	3	16
47	HR	7	4	7
48	HR	9	5	7
49	HR	5	5	19
50	Engineering	2	6	1
51	Sales	6	8	15
52	Engineering	8	9	5
53	HR	4	4	19
54	Marketing	5	3	16
55	Marketing	3	2	8
56	Engineering	6	5	9
57	Marketing	2	3	3
58	Sales	7	6	8
59	Engineering	3	3	4
60	HR	8	3	1
61	Engineering	3	5	15
62	Sales	1	9	13
63	Sales	4	9	9
64	HR	1	8	10
65	Engineering	9	8	5
66	Sales	2	5	16
67	HR	1	5	9
68	Sales	9	7	13
69	Engineering	2	3	13
70	Marketing	9	7	6
71	Marketing	5	8	5
72	Engineering	1	9	18
73	Engineering	6	3	19
74	Engineering	2	6	1
75	Engineering	9	4	7

Employee ID	Department	Satisfaction Score	Engagement Score	Tenure
76	HR	9	3	11
77	HR	7	8	1
78	Sales	4	3	2
79	Sales	1	5	6
80	HR	9	6	12
81	HR	9	3	12
82	Marketing	7	6	6
83	HR	4	2	6
84	HR	4	7	16
85	Engineering	6	1	14
86	HR	1	5	10
87	HR	2	6	9
88	Marketing	6	2	3
89	Marketing	5	7	9
90	Marketing	3	3	5
91	Marketing	8	5	19
92	Engineering	1	3	7
93	Engineering	1	2	9
94	HR	3	2	7
95	Marketing	6	5	11
96	Marketing	6	1	16
97	Engineering	7	4	19
98	HR	8	6	4
99	Marketing	7	5	9
100	Engineering	3	9	4

RETAIL SUCCESS METRICS

Overview: This dataset provides key metrics for retail stores, including fields such as `Store ID`, `Year`, `Revenue Growth`, `Customer Satisfaction`, and `Productivity Index`.

Use cases:

- *Trend analysis*: Examine revenue growth, customer satisfaction, and productivity over time to see which stores perform best.

- *Comparative analysis*: Compare performance metrics between stores to identify high-performing locations and strategies.
- *Dashboard creation*: Use this dataset to create a performance dashboard for monitoring retail success metrics in real time.

Store ID	Year	Revenue Growth	Customer Satisfaction	Productivity Index
1	2023	0.1	9	85.9
2	2022	0.06	5	67.57
3	2023	0.19	8	94.44
4	2021	0.2	8	67.07
5	2021	0.05	3	55.87
6	2022	0.12	9	52.37
7	2023	0.08	6	75.05
8	2021	0.06	9	92.66
9	2022	0.17	6	94.14
10	2021	0.06	9	68.48
11	2021	0.18	1	77.12
12	2023	0.18	9	80.4
13	2021	0.07	8	95.91
14	2023	0.02	1	50.18
15	2021	0.14	6	71.95
16	2021	0.17	6	59.91
17	2021	0.06	6	82.46
18	2023	0.12	7	76.45
19	2023	0.12	5	51.66
20	2021	0.07	6	53.29
21	2022	0.12	4	80.75
22	2021	0.12	1	91.88
23	2021	0.15	1	83.79
24	2022	0.05	1	92.65
25	2023	0.02	7	51.57
26	2022	0.02	1	61.41
27	2021	0.14	9	76.81
28	2021	0.08	6	74.71
29	2022	0.06	2	75.64

Store ID	Year	Revenue Growth	Customer Satisfaction	Productivity Index
30	2021	0.07	8	87.99
31	2022	0.2	7	70.94
32	2021	0.1	7	59.63
33	2022	0.16	5	92.9
34	2022	0.04	1	81.11
35	2022	0.04	5	71.76
36	2023	0.05	2	64.48
37	2022	0.08	8	96.21
38	2023	0.05	2	93.39
39	2023	0.18	7	52.56
40	2021	0.08	6	72.73
41	2022	0.14	2	61.66
42	2022	0.18	5	64.77
43	2022	0.11	8	85.27
44	2021	0.13	1	87.12
45	2022	0.13	2	96.07
46	2021	0.19	6	68.6
47	2021	0.13	7	78.03
48	2023	0.06	2	62.71
49	2023	0.17	7	87.55
50	2021	0.12	1	60.74
51	2023	0.03	3	77.62
52	2022	0.14	7	76.96
53	2022	0.18	3	64.41
54	2021	0.09	7	69.26
55	2023	0.17	8	92.29
56	2023	0.16	6	86.13
57	2022	0.05	2	86.19
58	2021	0.03	8	74.44
59	2022	0.13	4	76.31
60	2023	0.19	7	60.44
61	2022	0.17	1	62.26
62	2023	0.01	1	89.64

Store ID	Year	Revenue Growth	Customer Satisfaction	Productivity Index
63	2022	0.05	6	93.93
64	2023	0.03	3	80.56
65	2023	0.19	8	98.61
66	2023	0.05	5	50.67
67	2021	0.07	1	97.99
68	2021	0.08	3	92.38
69	2023	0.09	8	55.16
70	2021	0.11	5	75.8
71	2023	0.14	1	97.96
72	2021	0.05	4	90.11
73	2023	0.1	9	65.15
74	2021	0.01	5	80.97
75	2023	0.11	3	92.14
76	2021	0.09	6	57.45
77	2021	0.13	2	88.79
78	2021	0.11	9	96.88
79	2021	0.11	9	75.24
80	2023	0.1	4	57.98
81	2023	0.18	2	63.74
82	2021	0.08	2	60.05
83	2023	0.12	1	59.72
84	2023	0.15	6	50.05
85	2021	0.13	7	59.22
86	2021	0.11	8	57.98
87	2022	0.03	8	67.78
88	2022	0.09	6	57.48
89	2021	0.15	1	60.77
90	2021	0.08	6	94.97
91	2023	0.09	7	72.32
92	2023	0.14	4	64.29
93	2021	0.16	5	77.22
94	2023	0.04	3	52.36
95	2021	0.04	1	98.89

Store ID	Year	Revenue Growth	Customer Satisfaction	Productivity Index
96	2023	0.07	5	88.5
97	2023	0.18	5	65.99
98	2023	0.04	2	71.79
99	2022	0.07	9	87.78
100	2022	0.17	9	94.41

100 LUMINARIES IN DATA ANALYSIS

GENERAL

1. John Tukey (1915–2000)
Pioneered exploratory data analysis (EDA) and introduced innovations like the box plot and fast Fourier transform (FFT), foundational for data exploration.

2. Edward Tufte (1942–Present)
Known for The Visual Display of Quantitative Information, a key figure in data visualization, emphasizing clarity and integrity in design.

3. Hadley Wickham (1979–Present)
Revolutionized R with the tidyverse collection, including ggplot2 and dplyr, making data workflows simpler and more accessible.

4. Claudia Perlich (1975–Present)
Expert in predictive modeling in advertising, known for ethical, privacy-aware models and responsible data use.

5. DJ Patil (1974–Present)
The first U.S. chief data scientist, championed data for social good, focusing on health and justice reform.

6. Cathy O'Neil (1972–Present)
Author of Weapons of Math Destruction, advises on ethical data use, transparency, and fairness in predictive modeling.

7. Geoffrey Hinton (1947–Present)
"Godfather of Deep Learning," his work in neural networks led to advances in AI and computer vision.

8. Dean Abbott (1962–Present)

Co-founder of SmarterHQ, specializes in predictive analytics and data mining, with influential books on machine learning.

9. Peter Norvig (1956–Present)

Google Research Director and co-author of Artificial Intelligence: A Modern Approach, known for scalable search and NLP.

10. Leland Wilkinson (1944–2021)

Authored The Grammar of Graphics, foundational for data visualization theory and influencing modern graphics tools like ggplot2.

STATISTICS AND DATA SCIENCE

11. Ronald A. Fisher (1890–1962)

Founded modern statistics with contributions like ANOVA and maximum likelihood estimation.

12. Karl Pearson (1857–1936)

Established the Pearson correlation coefficient, foundational in statistical theory.

13. Jerzy Neyman (1894–1981)

Co-developed hypothesis testing, crucial for statistical inference.

14. William Gosset (1876–1937)

Developed Student's t-test under the pseudonym "Student," essential for small-sample testing.

15. George Box (1919–2013)

Known for Box-Jenkins models in time-series analysis and the Box-Cox transformation.

16. Bradley Efron (1938–Present)

Invented the bootstrap method, essential for resampling in statistical accuracy.

17. Francis Galton (1822–1911)

Introduced regression and correlation, critical for data relationships.

18. Andrey Kolmogorov (1903–1987)

Key figure in probability theory, laying a foundation for modern statistics.

19. C. R. Rao (1920–Present)

Advanced multivariate analysis, contributing to statistical methods used globally.

20. Yoshua Bengio (1964–Present)

Deep learning innovator, known for work on neural networks and representation learning.

MACHINE LEARNING AND ARTIFICIAL INTELLIGENCE

21. Yann LeCun (1960–Present)
Developed convolutional neural networks (CNNs), foundational in image recognition.

22. Michael I. Jordan (1956–Present)
Leader in Bayesian networks and machine learning theory.

23. Andrew Ng (1976–Present)
Co-founder of Coursera, popularizing AI and machine learning education.

24. David Silver (1975–Present)
Expert in reinforcement learning, known for his work at DeepMind.

25. Ian Goodfellow (1985–Present)
Invented generative adversarial networks (GANs), transformative in synthetic data generation.

26. Rich Sutton (1958–Present)
Co-author of Reinforcement Learning: An Introduction, advancing reinforcement learning theory.

27. Fei-Fei Li (1976–Present)
Visionary in computer vision, leading the influential ImageNet project.

28. Stuart Russell (1962–Present)
Co-author of Artificial Intelligence: A Modern Approach and advocate for AI ethics.

29. Tom Mitchell (1951–Present)
Machine learning pioneer and author of influential textbooks.

30. Daphne Koller (1968–Present)
Bayesian networks expert, co-founder of Coursera.

DATA VISUALIZATION AND COMMUNICATION

31. Ben Shneiderman (1947–Present)
Innovated dynamic query techniques, foundational in HCI and visualization.

32. William S. Cleveland (1943–Present)
Advanced statistical graphics with a focus on effective visualization methods.

33. Hans Rosling (1948–2017)
Co-founded Gapminder, a tool for visualizing global health trends and public health data.

34. David McCandless (1971–Present)
Founded Information is Beautiful, democratizing data storytelling.

35. Alberto Cairo (1974–Present)
Author of The Truthful Art and advocate for ethical data visualization.

36. Michael Friendly (1945–Present)
Worked on statistical graphics history, promoting visual data understanding.

37. Tamara Munzner (1968–Present)
Visualization theorist and author of Visualization Analysis and Design.

38. Jonathan Schwabish (1973–Present)
Economist and visualization expert known for accessible, complex data presentation.

39. Noah Iliinsky (1977–Present)
Visualization designer and co-author of Designing Data Visualizations.

40. Nathan Yau (1981–Present)
Creator of FlowingData, focused on accessible, insightful visualizations.

ETHICS AND POLICY IN DATA SCIENCE

41. Julia Angwin (1972–Present)
Journalist who exposed algorithmic biases, co-founder of The Markup.

42. Danah Boyd (1977–Present)
Data ethics researcher focused on social media, privacy, and youth.

43. Ruha Benjamin (1978–Present)
Author on racial biases in technology, promoting fair algorithmic practices.

44. Timnit Gebru (1983–Present)
AI ethics researcher known for work on bias in facial recognition.

45. Joy Buolamwini (1989–Present)
Founder of the Algorithmic Justice League, advocating against AI bias.

46. Kate Crawford (1973–Present)
Co-founder of The AI Now Institute, advancing AI ethics research.

47. Virginia Eubanks (1972–Present)
Author of Automating Inequality, critiquing biased data systems.

48. Shoshana Zuboff (1951–Present)
Author of The Age of Surveillance Capitalism, examining digital privacy.

49. Latanya Sweeney (1969–Present)
Data privacy researcher known for work on re-identification risks.

50. Meredith Broussard (1975–Present)
Critic of "technochauvinism" and author of Artificial Unintelligence.

DATA SCIENCE IN ACADEMIA AND RESEARCH

51. Jeffrey Heer (1978–Present)
Co-founder of Trifacta, providing advanced data-wrangling tools and visualization.

52. Sebastian Thrun (1967–Present)
Autonomous driving pioneer, led research at Google X.

53. Michael Stonebraker (1943–Present)
Database systems pioneer, influential in relational database theory.

54. Christopher Bishop (1959–Present)
Microsoft researcher and author of Pattern Recognition and Machine Learning.

55. John Kruschke (1956–Present)
Known for Bayesian data analysis.

56. Jerome Friedman (1939–Present)
Co-author of The Elements of Statistical Learning.

57. Trevor Hastie (1953–Present)
Co-author of foundational texts on statistical learning.

58. Robert Tibshirani (1956–Present)
Co-creator of the lasso, influential in statistical learning.

59. Leo Breiman (1928–2005)
Developed random forests, foundational in machine learning.

60. Alexandra Chouldechova (1985–Present)
Researcher focused on fairness and transparency in predictive models.

APPLIED DATA SCIENCE IN INDUSTRY

61. Hilary Mason (1978–Present)
Co-founder of Fast Forward Labs, known for practical applications of data science.

62. Eric Siegel (1968–Present)
Author of Predictive Analytics, a leading voice in data science education.

63. Chris Wiggins (1972–Present)
Chief data scientist at The New York Times, applying data science in journalism.

64. Jeff Hammerbacher (1983–Present)
Co-founder of Cloudera and early big data advocate.

65. Wes McKinney (1984–Present)
Creator of pandas, a key library for data manipulation in Python.

66. Monica Rogati (1981–Present)
Former VP of Data at Jawbone, specializes in consumer behavior analytics.

67. François Chollet (1985–Present)
Creator of Keras, an open-source neural network library.

68. Nathan Marz (1983–Present)
Invented the Lambda architecture for big data.

69. Dean Allemang (1959–Present)
Expert in semantic web and linked data applications.

70. Kirk Borne (1965–Present)
Data science advisor and advocate for data literacy and education.

PUBLIC HEALTH AND SOCIAL GOOD

71. Bill Gates (1955–Present)
Philanthropist and advocate for data-driven approaches in global health.

72. Emily Oster (1980–Present)
Economist known for data-driven analysis in parenting and health.

73. Lant Pritchett (1959–Present)
Development economist focused on data-informed policy for economic growth.

74. Jeffrey Sachs (1954–Present)
Economist using data for sustainable development and poverty alleviation.

75. Steven Levitt (1967–Present)
Co-author of Freakonomics, applying data analysis to social issues.

76. Rachel Glennerster (1965–Present)
Works on randomized controlled trials for poverty reduction in public policy.

77. Esther Duflo (1972–Present)
Nobel laureate, known for randomized trials in evaluating poverty interventions.

78. Michael Kremer (1964–Present)
Nobel laureate economist focused on development and poverty reduction.

79. Howard Friedman (1963–Present)
Public health expert, known for data-driven approaches to health metrics.

80. Christopher Murray (1961–Present)
Researcher in global health metrics, focusing on health and policy.

DATABASE AND BIG DATA TECHNOLOGIES

81. Alfred Aho (1941–Present)
Computer scientist and co-author of The Design and Analysis of Computer Algorithms.

82. Edgar F. Codd (1923–2003)
Invented the relational database model, foundational for modern database management.

83. Patricia Selinger (1948–Present)
Known for her work on relational database optimization.

84. Jim Gray (1944–2007)
Made major contributions to database transaction processing and distributed computing.

85. Peter Chen (1947–Present)
Developed the entity-relationship (ER) model for databases.

86. James Dixon (1967–Present)
Creator of the "data lake" concept, influential in big data architecture.

87. Martin Fowler (1963–Present)
Promoted agile software development and data engineering practices.

88. DJ Patil (1974–Present)
Known for co-creating LinkedIn's "People You May Know" feature and popularizing the role of data scientist.

89. Doug Cutting (1965–Present)
Creator of Hadoop, a foundational technology for big data processing.

90. Jeff Dean (1968–Present)
Google engineer instrumental in the development of MapReduce and Bigtable.

NEURAL NETWORKS AND DEEP LEARNING

91. Sepp Hochreiter (1967–Present)
Co-developed long short-term memory (LSTM) networks, foundational for time-series data.

92. Jürgen Schmidhuber (1963–Present)
Pioneer in recurrent neural networks, including LSTM.

93. Andrew Y. Ng (1976–Present)
Educator who co-founded Google Brain, popularized AI and machine learning education.

94. Alex Graves (1983–Present)

Known for advances in recurrent neural networks and applications in handwriting recognition.

95. Hugo Larochelle (1982–Present)

Deep learning researcher focusing on machine learning at Google Brain.

96. Yoshua Bengio (1964–Present)

Deep learning leader and co-recipient of the Turing Award for work on neural networks.

97. Ian Goodfellow (1985–Present)

Inventor of GANs, highly influential in generative modeling.

98. Christopher Manning (1965–Present)

NLP expert, known for Stanford NLP and advances in dependency parsing.

99. Yoav Goldberg (1980–Present)

Researcher in neural networks for NLP, known for work in deep learning applied to text.

100. Sebastian Ruder (1987–Present)

Researcher known for contributions to NLP, transfer learning, and multilingual models.

TOP 10 DATA-DRIVEN DECISIONS

1. Google's AdWords optimization: Redefining the advertising industry

   - *Background*: In the early 2000s, Google's search engine had already become a key online resource, but its business model was still evolving. Google AdWords, initially launched in 2000, relied on a pay-per-click model, which at first lacked significant targeting or optimization. The team realized, however, that through advanced data analysis, it could maximize ad relevance and performance, transforming online advertising from guesswork to a science.
   - *The data approach*: Google used click-through rates, historical ad performance, user profiles, and Web behavior data to optimize ads. The platform's algorithms analyzed which ads were most likely to receive clicks and conversions based on user intent inferred from search queries.
   - *Impact on industry*: This optimization model created a massive paradigm shift, turning online ads into a multi-billion-dollar industry. Google effectively became the pioneer of data-driven advertising, influencing every digital marketing platform that followed.
   - *Result*: Today, Google Ads, which AdWords was renamed in 2018, is one of the most profitable and influential advertising platforms, generating over $200 billion annually. This success cemented Google's position as a dominant force in the tech industry, with a business model that has yet to be rivaled in scope and profitability.

2. Amazon's recommendation engine: Personalized shopping at scale

   - *Background*: Amazon's founder, Jeff Bezos, envisioned a customer-centric model from the start, focusing on making it easy for people to find what they wanted quickly. The challenge was delivering personalized recommendations without manual curation, especially as the platform's product catalog rapidly expanded.

- *The data approach*: Amazon developed a collaborative filtering algorithm that analyzes purchase histories, browsing behavior, and product interaction data to make personalized recommendations. The algorithm evolved to include multiple factors, such as past purchases, cart additions, ratings, and wishlist items, which helped refine the suggestions even further.

- *Impact on industry*: Amazon's recommendation engine set a new standard in e-commerce, demonstrating the power of data to drive personalized customer experiences. The algorithm became so effective that customers felt Amazon "knew" them, enhancing engagement and increasing sales.

- *Result*: Amazon attributes up to 35% of its sales to its recommendation engine, making it one of the most effective data-driven systems in retail. The model influenced other platforms to adopt recommendation algorithms, including Netflix and Spotify.

3. Netflix's transition to streaming and original content creation

- *Background*: Initially, Netflix operated as a DVD rental service. In the late 2000s, the company noticed trends showing a decline in physical rentals and a surge in demand for instant access. By 2010, Netflix began using viewership data to predict and plan the transition to streaming.

- *The data approach*: Using detailed data on user preferences, viewing times, and engagement, Netflix identified the most popular genres, actors, and even specific storylines that resonated with audiences. This data not only guided the shift to streaming but later became the basis for investing in original content.

- *Impact on industry*: Netflix's approach to data-driven content creation with its first original series, *House of Cards*, was a breakthrough. By analyzing viewership data, they knew there was a ready audience for a political thriller. This data-guided strategy reshaped how content was developed, greenlit, and marketed.

- *Result*: Today, Netflix has over 200 million subscribers and has transformed the entertainment industry by popularizing streaming and leading with data-informed content decisions. The success of original content has inspired competing platforms such as Disney+ and Amazon Prime Video to invest heavily in data-driven content.

4. Walmart's disaster preparation using data analytics

- *Background*: Walmart is known for its operational efficiency and large-scale distribution network. When the company observed unusual demand spikes for certain products in hurricane-prone regions, they decided to leverage their sales data to understand these patterns.

- *The data approach*: Walmart analyzed historical sales data from stores in areas affected by hurricanes and other natural disasters, identifying high-demand items such as bottled water, batteries, and, surprisingly, items such as Pop-Tarts. The company used this insight to stock stores preemptively.
- *Impact on industry*: Walmart's proactive approach set a standard for disaster readiness in retail. By stocking essential items ahead of demand spikes, they helped communities stay prepared and made Walmart the go-to store in emergencies.
- *Result*: This data-driven decision has saved Walmart millions by ensuring products are available when and where they're most needed, maximizing sales during crisis periods and improving community trust.

5. UPS's ORION routing system: Optimizing delivery routes

- *Background*: As a logistics company, UPS incurs massive fuel and labor costs. The company recognized that even small efficiencies in routing could save millions. Thus, the On-Road Integrated Optimization and Navigation (ORION) system was developed.
- *The data approach*: ORION uses advanced algorithms and historical data on traffic patterns, package delivery times, and driver behaviors. It calculates the most efficient routes, minimizing left turns to reduce idling time and improving delivery speed.
- *Impact on industry*: UPS's ORION system redefined logistics and set a new standard for delivery efficiency. It showcased the potential of data-driven optimizations in cutting operational costs and environmental impact.
- *Result*: ORION saves UPS approximately 10 million gallons of fuel annually and reduces its carbon footprint by tens of thousands of metric tons, all while improving delivery speed.

6. Starbucks' data-driven location strategy with GIS analytics

- *Background*: Starbucks aimed to expand aggressively without cannibalizing its own market. Location is critical for any retail chain, and Starbucks needed a way to ensure new stores would thrive.
- *The data approach*: Starbucks uses geographic information system (GIS) and demographic data to assess potential locations. Factors such as foot traffic, population density, income levels, and proximity to other Starbucks locations are analyzed to predict store performance.
- *Impact on industry*: This data-driven site selection method has allowed Starbucks to scale efficiently. GIS technology in retail expansion has since been adopted widely, helping other chains to make data-informed location decisions.
- *Result*: Starbucks successfully established a global brand with over 30,000 locations, each strategically placed for maximum impact, thanks to its data approach.

7. Airbnb's dynamic pricing model

   - *Background*: To help hosts maximize earnings while meeting guest demand, Airbnb needed a way to optimize listing prices in real time. They found that static pricing often resulted in missed booking opportunities and lost revenue.
   - *The data approach*: Airbnb developed a machine learning–based dynamic pricing model that adjusts prices based on demand, local events, seasonality, and booking trends. The model suggests optimal prices to hosts to increase bookings.
   - *Impact on industry*: This dynamic pricing approach is now a common strategy in hospitality and travel. Hotels and airlines already used it, but Airbnb's model democratized it for individual property owners.
   - *Result*: Hosts who follow Airbnb's pricing suggestions tend to see higher occupancy rates and earnings, making Airbnb a more competitive option against traditional hotels.

8. Target's predictive analytics in personalized marketing

   - *Background*: Target's analytics team wanted to identify major life events in customers' lives, as they often trigger increased spending. Pregnancy, for example, drives purchases across many categories.
   - *The data approach*: Target used purchasing data to identify behavioral patterns, such as increased buying of unscented lotion, vitamins, and certain types of clothing, to predict pregnancy. This allowed them to send targeted ads for baby products before competitors.
   - *Impact on industry*: Target's predictive analytics methods were pioneering in personalized marketing. The approach set a new standard for retail personalization, though it also raised privacy concerns.
   - *Result*: The strategy boosted customer loyalty and sales but prompted public discourse on data privacy, pushing companies to be more transparent about data usage.

9. Ford's data-driven vehicle design for the Ford F-150

   - *Background*: As one of Ford's best-selling models, the F-150 is crucial to the company's success. Ford began using data to align vehicle features with customer needs, especially in the competitive truck market.
   - *The data approach*: Ford gathered data from customer feedback, survey responses, and driving habits to identify desired features. By analyzing this data, Ford optimized elements such as fuel efficiency, safety, and towing capacity to meet consumer demand.
   - *Impact on industry*: Ford's data-driven approach influenced other automakers to adopt customer-centric vehicle designs, focusing on utility and customization.

- *Result*: The F-150 has remained the best-selling truck in the United States for over four decades, demonstrating the effectiveness of data-driven product design.

10. City of Los Angeles' data-driven crime prevention efforts

    - *Background*: The Los Angeles Police Department (LAPD) sought a more efficient way to prevent crime. They developed a predictive policing program that uses data to anticipate crime hotspots.
    - *The data approach*: The LAPD analyzed historical crime data, applying algorithms to predict where crimes were likely to occur. This information enabled more targeted resource deployment in high-risk areas.
    - *Impact on industry*: Predictive policing models have been adopted in several major cities, though they remain controversial for potential biases. Nonetheless, it highlighted the use of data in public policy.
    - *Result*: The LAPD reported reductions in certain crime rates.

A

Advanced artificial intelligence (AI),
    101–102
Aggregated data, 23
Agile approach, 91
Airbnb, 168
Algorithm, 6
    clustering, 48, 50, 56
    fairness, bias, and transparency in, 60–62,
        70, 71
    machine learning, 12, 18, 47, 94, 102, 105
    supervised, 50
Algorithmic fairness, 61, 122
Amazon™, 88, 165–166
Anomaly detection, 12, 55, 56
ANOVA (Analysis of Variance), 20, 28, 29
Anti-discrimination laws, 62–63
Application programming interface (API),
    3–4, 17
Artificial intelligence (AI), 5, 70, 89,
    101–102, 105, 106, 122
Association rule mining, 52
Augmented analytics, 102, 105
Augmented reality (AR), 104
Autoencoders, 48
AutoML (automated machine learning),
    103, 105

B

Bell curve, 20
Bias detection and mitigation, 61–62

Binomial distribution, 20
Blockchain technology, for data integrity,
    104
Bootstrapping, 49
Business intelligence (BI) tools, 34
Business strategies. *see also* Data-driven
        decision-making
    data-driven decision-making
        concepts and terminology, 7
        decision support, 6
        lifecycle optimization, 6–7

C

California Consumer Privacy Act (CCPA),
    103, 106
Case studies
    e-commerce, predictive analytics and
        machine learning, 50–54
    financial services industry, 64–68
    healthcare organization, data literacy in,
        78–82
    manufacturing, predictive maintenance
        in, 22–26
    retail expansion, market trend analysis for,
        37–41
    specified industries, data-driven success,
        92–93
        compilation of, 93–96
        finance, 89
        healthcare, 89
        manufacturing, 89

marketing, 89
retail, 88–89
supply chain operations, 7–11
Categorical data, 19
Categorical variables, 18, 20
Chi-square tests, 20, 29
Clustering algorithms, 48
Clustering techniques, 19, 148
Confusion matrix, 4, 50
Correlation analysis, 16, 19, 29, 138
Correlation matrix, 19, 21, 24
Cross-validation techniques, 46, 49

D
Dashboard design principles, 34–35
Data acquisition, 3–4, 55
techniques of, 17
Data analysis
100 luminaries in, 157–164
hypothesis testing, 20
implementation roadmap, 28–29
probability distributions, 20
regression analysis, 20
statistical inference, 21
Data analytics
development of, 109–110
future of, 101–107
python for, 111–112
setting up and running, 109, 112–113
Data cleaning, 17–18, 27
Data collection
acquisition techniques, 17
ethical considerations in
fairness, mitigating bias and
transparency, 61–64
financial services industry, 64–68
implementation roadmap, 69–71
legal and regulatory frameworks,
62–63, 64
overview of, 59–60
and usage, 60–61, 63
implementation roadmap, 26–27
overview of, 15–16
quality and integrity, 17
source of, 16–17
Data communication, 159–160
data visualization and, 36–37
implementation roadmap, 41–43
overview of, 31–32

retail expansion, market trend analysis for,
37–41
strategies for, 35–36
Data-driven culture
data literacy
continuous learning, 75
education and training, 74–75
firsthand experience, 75
healthcare organization, 78–82
leadership support and sponsorship, 75
future of analytics, 106
implementation roadmap, 82–85
organizational challenges
change management programs, 75
data integration and governance, 75–76
key performance indicators and
metrics, 76
resource allocation, 76
overview of, 73–74
using analytics and building, 77–78
Data-driven decision-making
business strategies
concepts and terminology, 7
decision support, 6
lifecycle optimization, 6–7
concepts and terminologies, 5–6
data science lifecycle
block diagram of, 3
data acquisition, 3–4
data preparation, 4
deployment and monitoring, 4
development model, 4
evaluation model, 4
exploratory data analysis, 4
decision makers, 91–92
evolution of, 105
foundational principles of, 2–3
implementation of, 76–77
implementation roadmap, 11–13
overview of, 1–2
supply chain optimization, 7–11
Data-driven organizations
Airbnb, 168
Amazon, 165–166
Ford, 168–169
Google, 165
Los Angeles Police Department, 169
Netflix, 166
Starbucks, 167

Target, 168
UPS ORION, 167
Walmart, 166–167
Data-driven success
  decision-makers
    continuous improvement, 92
    impact and return on investment, 92
    leadership support, 91
    talent acquisition and development,
      91–92
  implementation roadmap, 96–99
  industry-specific case studies, 93–96
    finance, 89
    healthcare, 89
    manufacturing, 89
    marketing, 89
    retail, 88–89
  lessons learned and best practices
    agile and iterative approach, 91
    cross-functional collaboration, 90
    data quality and governance, 90
    ethical considerations, 91
  overview of, 87–88
Data ethics. *see also* Ethics, in data
      collection and usage
  future of analytics, 105–106
  and policy, 160
  privacy, and governance, 103
Data governance, 69–70, 84, 90, 105–106
Data integration, 18, 27
  and governance, 75–76
Data literacy
  continuous learning, 75
  education and training, 74–75
  firsthand experience, 75
  healthcare organization, 78–82
  leadership support and sponsorship, 75
Data ownership rights, 63
Data preparation, 4, 46–47, 102
Data preprocessing
  cleaning, 17–18
  implementation roadmap, 26–27
  integration, 18
  transformation, 18
Data quality assurance, 21
Data science foundations
  inference and prediction, 22
  pattern recognition, 21
  quality assurance, 21

Data science lifecycle
  block diagram of, 3
  data acquisition, 3–4
  data preparation, 4
  deployment and monitoring, 4
  development model, 4
  evaluation model, 4
  exploratory data analysis, 4
Dataset(s)
  business sales and marketing, 131–134
  city pollution levels, 138–141
  credit risk assessment, 144–148
  employee engagement survey, 148–151
  housing sale prices, 141–144
  retail success metrics, 151–155
  retail transactions, 134–137
Data storytelling, 34, 36–37
Data transformation, 18, 55
Data visualization, 159–160
  and data communication, 36–37
  implementation roadmap, 41–43
  overview of, 31–32
  principles of, 32–33
  retail expansion, market trend analysis for,
    37–41
  techniques of, 19, 27–28
  tools and techniques for, 33–35
Deep learning, 102, 163–164
Dimensionality reduction techniques, 18,
    19, 48

E
E-commerce, predictive analytics and
    machine learning, 50–54
Edge computing, 102, 105
Education and training, in data literacy, 75
Empowering decision-makers, 107
Equipment monitoring, 22, 25, 26, 126
Ethical frameworks, 121–123
Ethics and policy, in data science, 160
Ethics, in data collection and usage
  algorithms and machine learning
    bias detection and mitigation, 61–62
    fairness, 61
    impact assessments, 62
    transparency and explainability, 62
  data security, 61
  description of, 59–60
  implementation roadmap, 69–71

legal and regulatory frameworks
   anti-discrimination laws, 62–63
   data ownership rights, 63
   intellectual property rights, 63
   protection laws and regulations, 62
   regulatory compliance, 63
  ownership and control rights, 60–61
  privacy and consent, 60
  responsible data usage, 61
  using data analytics, 63–64
Exploratory data analysis (EDA), 2, 4, 134
  clustering techniques, 19
  correlation analysis, 19
  descriptive statistics, 18–19
  dimensionality reduction techniques, 19
  objectives of, 27–28
  predictive maintenance in manufacturing,
   23
  visualization techniques, 19
External APIs, 17

F
Fairness-aware techniques, 61
Financial services industry
  data-driven success, 89
  data ethics, 64–68
Firsthand experience, in data literacy, 75
Ford, 168–169
Foundations of data science
  inference and prediction, 22
  pattern recognition, 21
  quality assurance, 21
F1-score, 49, 50, 56
Future of data analytics, 101–107

G
General Data Protection Regulation
  (GDPR), 103, 106
General Electric™, 88, 89
Geographic information systems (GIS), 34
Google, 17, 165
Graphics processing units (GPUs), 110
Grid search, 52

H
Healthcare industry
  data-driven success, 89
  data literacy, 78–82
Hierarchical clustering, 19, 48, 56
Histograms, 19, 21, 23, 67

Holdout dataset, 49, 56
Hyperparameter tuning, 4, 103
Hypothesis testing, 20, 22, 29

I
IBM Watson Health™, 88, 89
Immersive visualization technologies, 104
Infographics, and data storytelling, 34
Insight communication, 36
Integrated development environments
  (IDEs), 109, 110
Intellectual property rights, 63
Interactive data visualizations, 33
Interactive exploration, 36
Internet of Things (IoT), 94, 104
Iterative approach, 88, 91

J
Jupyter Notebook, 109, 110, 112, 113

K
Key performance indicators (KPIs), 76
K-fold cross-validation, 49
K-means clustering, 19, 48, 56

L
Legal and regulatory frameworks
  anti-discrimination laws, 62–63
  data ownership rights, 63
  intellectual property rights, 63
  protection laws and regulations, 62
  regulatory compliance, 63
Libraries, data visualization, 33–34
Lifecycle of data science
  block diagram of, 3
  data acquisition, 3–4
  data preparation, 4
  deployment and monitoring, 4
  development model, 4
  evaluation model, 4
  exploratory data analysis, 4
Logistic regression, 20
Los Angeles Police Department, 169

M
Machine learning (ML)
  advanced AI and, 101–102
  algorithm, 12, 18, 47, 94, 102, 105
  and artificial intelligence, 159
  AutoML, 103

e-commerce, 50–54
implementation roadmap, 54–57
overfitting and underfitting, 49
overview of, 45–46
predictive analytics and, 50
supervised and unsupervised learning, 47–48, 55–56
Manufacturing industry, data-driven success of, 89
Marketing industry, data-driven success of, 89
Matplotlib, 111–112
Mean squared error (MSE), 49
Model development, 4
Model evaluation
data science lifecycle, 4
predictive modeling, 47
and validation, 48–49
predictive analytics and machine learning, 50
supervised and unsupervised learning techniques, 48–49
Model evaluation and validation, predictive modeling, 48–49, 50
Monte Carlo simulation, 49

N
Natural language processing (NLP), 102
Netflix™, 88, 90, 166
Neural networks, 102, 163–164
NumPy, 111

O
Organizational challenges, data-driven culture
change management programs, 75
data integration and governance, 75–76
key performance indicators and metrics, 76
resource allocation, 76
Overfitting, 49

P
Pandas, 111
Pattern recognition, 21
PayPal™, 88, 89
Performance metrics, 10, 49
Persuasive data storytelling, 37–38
Poisson distribution, 20
Polynomial regression, 20

Precision, 49, 50, 56
Predictive analytics, 5–6
e-commerce, 50–54
implementation roadmap, 54–57
and machine learning, 50
in manufacturing, 22–26
modeling process, 50
data preparation, 46–47
evaluation and validation, 48–49
problem formulation, 46
selection, training, evaluation and deployment, 47
Principal component analysis (PCA), 18, 19, 48
Probability distributions, 20, 22
Protection laws and regulations, 62
Python
codings and explanations, 125–130
for data analytics environment, 109–113
library, 33–34
scripts
e-commerce, predictive analytics and machine learning, 54
financial services industry, 68
healthcare organization, data literacy in, 78–82
predictive maintenance, 25–26
retail expansion, market trend analysis for, 40–41
using retail industry, 10–11

Q
Quantum computing, 103–104

R
Rank correlation, 19
Raw data, cleaning and transforming, 17–18
Real-time data analytics, 23, 94, 102, 106
Regression analysis, 20, 22
Regression modeling, 20, 29, 48
Regularization techniques, 49
Regulatory compliance, 63
Retail expansion, market trend analysis for, 37–41
Retail industry, data-driven success of, 88–89
Retail supply chain operations, 7–8
Return on investment (ROI), 92
Root mean squared error (RMSE), 49
R-squared (R^2), 49

S
Scaling features, 18
Scatter plots, 19
Scikit-learn, 112
Seaborn, 111–112, 126
Spearman rank correlation, 19
Starbucks, 167
Statistical fundamentals, of data analysis
   hypothesis testing, 20
   implementation roadmap, 28–29
   probability distributions, 20
   regression analysis, 20
   statistical inference, 21
Statistical inference, 16, 21
Strategic asset, 106
Stratified cross-validation, 49
Supervised learning techniques, 45, 47–48,
   55–56
Supply chain operations, 7–11

T
Target, 168

T-distributed stochastic neighbor
   embedding (t-SNE), 19, 48
Transparency, fairness, bias and, 61–62

U
Underfitting, 49
Unsupervised learning techniques, 45,
   47–48, 50, 55–56
UPS ORION, 167

V
Virtual reality (VR), 104
Visual Studio Code (VS Code), 109, 110

W
Walmart, 166–167
Web scraping, 4, 16, 17

X
X (formerly Twitter), 17

www.ingramcontent.com/pod-product-compliance
Lightning Source LLC
LaVergne TN
LVHW022314060326
832902LV00020B/3454

9 781501 523311